Contents

DESIGNING FOR CHILDREN WITH SPECIAL EDUCATIONAL NEEDS
Ordinary Schools

Department of Education and Science

Building Bulletin 61

London: Her Majesty's Stationery Office

Figures

Key to symbols used in the Figures

pupil chair

teacher chair

rocking chair

adult arm chair

stool

seat cube

bench seat (1200mm)

bench seat (1500mm)

bench seat (1800mm)

table

table

table

table

science bench

teacher's desk

teacher's wall cupboard

workbench

carrel

secondary practical table

practical table with cupboard

secondary individual table

carpeted area

paper trolley

book trolleys

coats trolley

trolleys with trays

trolley (6 trays)

storage trolleys

cupboard trolley

trolley with display back

service trolleys

mobile bin

traycart

overhead projector trolley

fc filing cabinet

book or display shelves (900mm)

book shelves (600mm)

storage divider units

storage divider units

sink and drainer

art sink

sand and water trolley

drainer trolley

easel

Abbreviations

A	wheelchair access		m	mirror
CCTV	closed-circuit television		ohp	overhead projector
cpd	cupboard		s	sink
d	drier		sh	shower
fc	filing cabinet		st	store
fr	fridge		T	telephone
fr door	fire-resisting door		w	washing machine
lb	lavatory basin			

Note on measurements

Where dimensions are given in the figures as '750', '900' etc these are *minimum* dimensions in millimetres, and where given as '750mm' etc are exact measurements (eg of standard furniture). Room dimensions are given in metres.

1.   Introduction

1.1   The education of children with special needs is currently provided for in a variety of types of school and unit. In recent years the international climate of opinion has tended towards the view that, for as many children as possible, this education should be provided in local, mainstream schools rather than separate special establishments. Section 2 of the Education Act 1981 reinforced the principle that, so far as is reasonably practicable, a child for whom special education is deemed to be appropriate should be educated in an ordinary school and be associated in the activities of the school with other children.

1.2   When a child's educational difficulties are such that it is considered necessary for the local education authority (LEA) concerned to make a statement[1] of his or her special educational needs, the decision on where educational provision is to be made depends on a number of factors. These include the views of parents and professional advisers and the ability of a school to meet a child's needs without detracting from the educational provision for other children in the school.

1.3   The number of children with special educational needs who are being educated in mainstream schools is gradually increasing, and this policy can be expected to continue. Many LEAs are reviewing their building stock as a whole, at a time when rolls are falling and space is becoming available, in order to make the most of their resources. This provides an opportunity to assess at the same time whether the accommodation available in their ordinary schools is suitable, or could be made so, for a population which includes children with special educational needs.

1.4   The accommodation available at present is not always suitable. The provision made is often in separate, temporary accommodation, or in an unsuitable location in the school, so that it is difficult for the children concerned to participate in all the activities of the school. It is hoped that such provision can be improved at the earliest opportunity.

1.5   The purpose of this document is to provide guidance on the ways in which ordinary school buildings can be used or adapted to meet the requirements of children with special educational needs, and how new primary and secondary schools can be designed to meet these requirements. It looks both at the range of accommodation required and at the school environment as a whole, and provides specific guidance for a range of different disabilities and needs. It should be of use where remodelling of existing buildings or replacement with new is being considered, and also as a guide to where minor adaptations are necessary. The implications for the capacity of existing schools are also discussed.

1.6   It is hoped that this guidance will be of particular assistance to LEA advisers, education officers and architects in early discussions and the preparation of a brief. Some of the material may also be helpful to headteachers and teaching staff in their organisation and use of buildings and individual spaces.

1.7   This study was prepared by a team comprising members of Architects and Building Group and Her Majesty's Inspectorate (HMI). The recommendations made are based on observations of good practice in the education of children with special needs in primary, secondary and special schools. The team received valuable help from special education advisers, headteachers, staff and pupils, and are most grateful to all of them.

---

1.   See *Assessments and Statements of Special Educational Needs.* Circular 1/83 (DES), HC(83)3/LAC(83)2(DHSS).

2. Scope of This Study

2.1 The accommodation required in a particular school or group of schools should be the subject of discussions involving a number of parties. These discussions must first consider the range of special educational needs to be provided for, how the LEA wishes to organise this provision, the suitability of its buildings, and in a particular school, the existing organisation and approach.

2.2 Although this study looks at how children with special educational needs can best be accommodated in ordinary schools, there is no intention to imply that special schools will no longer be needed. There will always be children for whom education in a special school is appropriate, and the need for LEAs to have access to all types of provision is discussed in Chapter 3.

2.3 The principles embodied in the 1981 Education Act are based on the concept of special educational need rather than on handicap. The focus is on the child rather than on his or her disability, and on his or her special educational needs in terms of abilities and interaction with the environment, rather than on the cause of those needs. It moves away from the categorisation of children into two groups: the handicapped and the non-handicapped, recognising that, at some point in their schooling, large numbers of children may need assistance in overcoming educational difficulties, whether mild or severe, however they are caused.

2.4 Although it is misleading to speak of 'categories', a broad grouping has been adopted for this Building Bulletin to describe those children with special educational needs for whom education in the ordinary school may be suitable. A building and its environment may further or hinder the teaching of pupils with a particular disability, and thus aspects specific to a particular need can usefully be grouped together. The four groupings of special educational needs covered by this Building Bulletin are:

(i) children with moderate learning difficulties

(ii) children with sensory handicaps

(iii) children with emotional and behavioural disorders

(iv) children with physical disabilities.

Children with speech and language disorders are also included, and because their needs in terms of accommodation are similar to those of groups (i) and (ii), they are placed after group (ii) in the text.

2.5 These groupings are only intended as a guide, as many children have more complex disabilities. Some of the children in groups (ii), (iii) and (iv) may have special educational needs similar to those with moderate learning difficulties. The degree of disability may also vary widely. It is therefore not feasible to give precise guidance on what to provide for any individual child: but the general recommendations made here will make it possible to accommodate whatever staff, teaching resources and equipment may be required to meet the child's special needs.

2.6 There may be children other than those described above for whom provision in the ordinary school might be made. Where it is appropriate to provide for pupils with more severe and complex learning difficulties, accommodation suitable for their curriculum needs should be designed in accordance with the suggestions for various ages and stages discussed in Design Note 10.[1] Opportunities for them to participate in the life of the school should be borne in mind in the design of the building.

Scale of provision

2.7 To give an idea of the scale of provision that may be required, it may be helpful to indicate the number of pupils involved. As this publication is primarily about building, it pays considerable attention to the needs of those children for whom the overall environment of a building is extremely important – that is, those with physical and sensory disabilities. However, these groups are relatively small in number. In January 1981 special educational provision was being made for about 12,000 children with sensory handicap and 19,000 with physical disability out of a total school population of 8,720,000. They are both therefore minority groups, and few children in either group are likely to be found together in one school. In the case of children with sensory handicaps a compromise must be reached that aims to make the best use of specialist teachers but to avoid making children travel long distances to schools just so that they can be grouped together. As far as physically disabled children are concerned, a useful indicator of likely distribution is that if every child formerly (ie before the 1981 Act) described as physically

1. *Designing for the Severely Handicapped.* Design Note 10, Architects and Building Group, Department of Education and Science, 1972.

handicapped could attend his or her local school, which is not necessarily the case, there would be one such child in every other primary school and one in every secondary school. With adequate access and some special teaching equipment and furniture, these children will be able to participate fully in the life of the school. For some, a small scale base for medical treatment may be required. Others may need access to support spaces if they have special learning needs.

2.8 Of those needing special educational provision, the largest number of children is those with moderate learning difficulties. The range of accommodation illustrated in this document therefore includes support centres for a comparatively large number, particularly in secondary schools, where there are more children identified as having moderate learning difficulties than at primary level. It should also be remembered that an estimated 20 per cent of the total school population[1] need special educational provision at some point in their school lives, and that the provision for pupils with moderate learning difficulties will also be a resource for those pupils in the school with milder learning difficulties (see also paragraph 4.10).

How to use this Building Bulletin

2.9 Chapters 4–7 of this document describe the range of accommodation that would be suitable for children with special needs in ordinary schools, both in terms of additional support space[2] and in terms of accommodation throughout the school. A suitable overall school design enables children to spend an appropriate proportion of their time in mainstream classes, and it is stressed throughout that the aim should be for these children to participate as fully as possible in the life of the whole school. It will be seen that a well-designed modern school goes a long way towards providing the desired environment, if suitable support provision can be made. Accommodation, however, is only one factor when assessing the suitability of a school for admitting children with special needs; the school's organisation

and approach, its resources, and its curriculum, are equally important.

2.10 Because numbers and degrees of need vary so greatly, and because LEAs will be operating in very different circumstances, a wide range of solutions is needed to meet varying requirements. This document therefore cannot be too prescriptive. It provides guidance for each stage of the briefing process, once educational needs have been assessed; it does not prescribe set solutions, and should be seen as a source of information to be drawn on as required. The design studies in Chapters 5–7 offer a degree of flexibility in use, to meet educational developments, changes in sizes of groups, etc.

2.11 *Chapter 4* is the first point of reference for the specific requirements of the groups of need outlined above. For each of the groups, a brief outline of educational needs is given. The accommodation requirements specific to each group are then summarised.

2.12 Where some of the children who are physically disabled also have additional learning difficulties, reference will need to be made to more than one section to assess accommodation needs. The chapter therefore provides a basic checklist of design requirements, both for the individual child and for a number of children.

2.13 The examples in *Chapters 5–7* should be drawn on for further detail on how best to put these design requirements into practice where support provision is necessary. They show a range of support spaces suitably equipped and furnished for primary and secondary schools. The ideas contained in the examples can be used both in adapting existing buildings or where new building is being considered, and cover a range of degrees of need from which it should be possible to select what is most appropriate in the circumstances. The plans and descriptions should be studied together with the recommendations of Chapter 4.

2.14 Chapter 5 includes examples of nursery schools and classes suitable for accommodating children with special needs. In Chapter 6 (primary school accommodation) the examples of support spaces are followed by a description of the supportive features of the school as a whole, with examples to illustrate the points made. In secondary schools, what is required in accommodation terms depends much more on the organisation and curriculum; and in Chapter 7, following the examples, the range of ingredients in secondary school design that best support the education of children with special needs are discussed.

2.15 At the end of Chapters 6 and 7, access for the physically disabled to practical, specialist subject and general teaching areas is considered and examples

---

1. *Special Educational Needs*. Report of the Committee of Enquiry into the Education of Handicapped Children and Young People (Warnock Report). HMSO, 1978.

2. The word 'support' is used in this document to cover the range of assistance which will be required by pupils with special educational needs in the ordinary school, as described in paragraphs 4.2–5. The terms 'support space' and 'support accommodation' are used to cover generally any kinds of space used for support to special needs teaching, often described elsewhere as 'special needs resource centres'. 'Support centre' is used here to denote a larger group of spaces, supporting special needs teaching and a wider range of activities than a support classroom or other area.

given. Further details on provision for the physically disabled will be found in the Appendix.

2.16   *Chapter 8* is a guide to the accommodation that will be required for health care, medical examination and the work of visiting specialists.

2.17   The enrolment of children with special educational needs has implications for the area of the whole school, and *Chapter 9* suggests ways of making appropriate space allowances. The space requirements are of two kinds. First, additional space may be required for support spaces. Second, whether or not support spaces are being provided, extra space must be allowed in the ordinary teaching spaces and for circulation around the school.

3. Range of Educational Provision for Children with Special Educational Needs

3.1 The full range of provision required to meet special educational needs includes the following:

(i) education in an ordinary class, with any necessary aids or support, sometimes including periods of withdrawal for special help;

(ii) education in the ordinary school, with a proportion of time spent in a special group or class;

(iii) education in a special school, with some shared lessons or social contact with a neighbouring ordinary school;

(iv) full-time education in an ordinary school or special day school with hostel nearby;

(v) full-time education in a special boarding school.

3.2 The full range of provision should be available to an LEA, whether or not all the types of provision are within its boundary, so that the most suitable placement for each child can be found. For some pupils, particularly some of those who are emotionally and behaviourally disturbed, boarding school placement or other residential support is essential.

3.3 This Building Bulletin is devoted to items (i) and (ii) above, that is, provision for special educational needs in the ordinary school. However, it is worth discussing here some of the implications of the special school/ordinary school link.

3.4 Where a special school is sited near a primary or secondary school it is possible for the ordinary school to be seen as an additional resource for some of the special school's pupils. For a primary or secondary school to be able to receive special school pupils in this way the building should meet the criteria described in the following chapters. For example, access for pupils in wheelchairs into and around the school and within the relevant teaching spaces should be provided, and for pupils with sensory handicaps the accommodation and its environment should be suitable.

3.5 Conversely the special school can become a resource of expertise, equipment or learning material for pupils with special educational needs in the ordinary school, and may also be a base for the peripatetic service to a number of schools. To serve as a central resource, the special school may need particular kinds of accommodation: for example, a pre-school home/school link may require a base for peripatetic staff to write and keep records and use telephones, somewhere to have discussions with parents, and perhaps a small playroom. The development of 'in-service' links with teachers from other schools may be helped by a suitable space for talks, and a teachers' workshop where equipment, aids and special teaching material can be seen, discussed and developed. A central resource for the service to hearing impaired pupils may be needed which would include an audiometry room and technicians' workshop. Many of the latter of course already exist either in a special school or elsewhere.

4. Accommodation Requirements in Ordinary Schools

4.1   This chapter describes the support that will be required by children with special educational needs in the ordinary school. Educational provision will range from ordinary class teaching, with special facilities provided as necessary, through individual or small group teaching, to teaching in a special environment in a larger group: in all cases additional space of some kind will be required. The accommodation requirements for each group are set out in the rest of this chapter; a summary of the most common points is given in paragraphs 4.2–8. The descriptions of the range of educational provision that may be made by an LEA or by a school to meet special needs are by no means exhaustive, but include any provision which may have a direct bearing on space, services or environment.

Summary of provision

4.2   Within the ordinary teaching situation, support for the pupil may include:

- use of special equipment or curriculum material

- assistance from a teacher on the staff who is responsible for special needs, or a peripatetic teacher or adviser, either directly or through the class or subject teacher

- use of special aids that enable a pupil to overcome or minimise a particular disability

- assistance to the pupil from aides (ancillary staff) in performing certain tasks.

4.3   An additional requirement, essential in many cases, is to be able to take children out of the ordinary class for short periods of time with a special teacher, either individually or in a small group.

4.4   Some pupils will need to spend a proportion of their time being taught in a group of between six and ten pupils in a specially assigned place. The amount of time spent in such a support group will vary according to the pupil's needs. Traditionally, such arrangements were variously described as 'special classes' or as 'designated units'. In some instances pupils spent all their time in such a group. It is hoped that the range of special provision made will be seen as a support to the enrolment of children in mainstream classes, rather as a separate specialist facility to which children are admitted.

4.5   For physically handicapped pupils certain access requirements have to be met; and for children with sensory handicaps, the overall environment of the school has to be considered as well as the acoustic and visual qualities of any support spaces provided. The information contained in this chapter should be read in conjunction with the requirements described in DES Design Notes 17, 18 and 25.[1]

4.6   The support accommodation required for each group is listed below as a range of requirements: the amount and nature of provision will vary according to the numbers to be provided for and the degree of their learning difficulty. In some cases the provision of a preparation room/store and a small quiet/tutorial room for extraction of an individual or small group will be adequate. At the other end of the spectrum, in a large secondary school a five- or six-teacher support centre for a large number of pupils with moderate learning difficulties may be necessary. It is unlikely that there will be full-scale support centres for more than one group of children with special educational needs in the same school. However, various combinations, such as a centre for pupils with moderate learning difficulties and provision for a small group of pupils with emotional and behavioural disorders, could be accommodated in a large secondary school.

4.7   As discussed in paragraph 2.10, it is not a simple matter, and may not be appropriate, to stipulate the exact number of pupils to be catered for by support accommodation. Where children are brought together for special needs teaching, the nominal group sizes will range from six to ten, depending upon type of special need, age, and degree of difficulty. The sizes of support spaces are similar, however, because smaller sized groups tend to consist of pupils who require slightly more space. Where approximate numbers for a support space are given below, the numbers are work places, and not the maximum number it could be supporting in a school, as the latter depends on staffing and organisation.

4.8   Descriptions to be found in Chapters 6, 7 and 9 such as 'a two-teacher centre' mean that the accommodation could be worked with a minimum of two teachers. There may of course be other adults working with them, and additional teachers who may for part of the time be supporting pupils with special educational needs in mainstream classes.

---

1.   *Guidelines for Environmental Design and Fuel Conservation in Educational Buildings.* Design Note 17, DES, 1981.
   Access for the Physically Disabled to Educational Buildings. Design Note 18, DES, 1979. (Revised edition in preparation.)
   Lighting and Acoustic Criteria for the Visually Handicapped and Hearing Impaired in Schools. Design Note 25, DES, 1981.

Use of support spaces

4.9   Where support centres are provided, it may be possible in certain cases for them to be used as a resource by other children with special needs as well as the group for whom they are designed, at times when part of the accommodation is free. All the designs for support centres for children with moderate learning difficulties shown in Chapters 6 and 7 are intended to serve as a resource for a number of other children with milder learning difficulties at different times. The back-up practical facilities provided in the centre may be available at times to other children with special needs. Where such extended use is appropriate, it is mentioned below under details of the support provision for each group.

Children with moderate learning difficulties

4.10   As already mentioned (paragraph 2.8), the largest group of children needing special educational provision is of those with moderate learning difficulties. Some of these children may have associated mild physical and sensory disabilities, and social and emotional difficulties, as well as limited general ability. The number of children identified as having moderate learning difficulties is greater at secondary than at primary level, and support provision must take this into account. The provision made for these pupils will serve as a resource for other children in the school with milder or short-term learning difficulties, and designs should also allow for the fact that children with physical disabilities may have associated moderate learning difficulties and may therefore also be using this provision.

Educational needs – primary level

4.11   Within the ordinary class, some children may benefit from access to special equipment and curriculum material. They may need help from an additional teacher (on the staff or peripatetic) responsible for children with special educational needs. These children may spend varying proportions of their time out of the ordinary class, in individual or small group teaching, or in a special group, in which the whole range of appropriate activities can be provided.

Accommodation requirements – primary level

Ordinary class bases

4.12   These will be most supportive if they have the facilities to be found in many well-designed, modern primary schools, as described in paragraphs 6.42–43.

Small story group in an infant school quiet bay

Support space

4.13   Depending on numbers and individual needs, the range of support space might include one or more of the following:

- if not already available, a small central preparation room for adults to prepare learning material, and to adapt and store special equipment (see Figure 4)
- a small quiet/tutorial room (see Figure 5)
- an individual study bay area, perhaps adjacent to the library
- a small group room specifically equipped for the use of learning aids (see Figure 6)
- a support space large enough for one support group, where a variety of activities can take place
- a support centre for two or more such groups.

4.14   There is an advantage in having at least two support groups, for instance in a JMI (ie a 5–11 primary school), and thus providing for them in a centre, as this makes it possible for a wider range of facilities and resources to be provided, and makes it easier for teachers to give support tailored to the children's ages and abilities.

Support centre

4.15   For the range of activities appropriate to these children, this should include:

- a base for each group, comprising general teaching area and practical facilities in or adjacent to it
- a small quiet bay or room off the general learning area, for story telling or quiet work
- a tutorial room for individual teaching, doubling as an 'office' for record-keeping, discussion with

staff, parents, peripatetic teachers and paramedical staff

- lockable storage for audiovisual aids and teaching equipment
- sufficient socket outlets for use of aids and equipment
- convenient lavatory accommodation which may need to be supplemented by facilities to shower a pupil in privacy
- access to common paved areas for outdoor work and play, with perhaps an area nearby for practising ball-handling skills and a low wall for practising balance and agility skills.

4.16   Examples of how support centres may be provided are given in Figures 7 and 8.

Individual teaching for a junior pupil using a microcomputer

Location of support centres

4.17   Whether in a new design or an adaptation of an existing school, the aim should be to site the support centre well within the body of the school rather than as an end-on addition or separate building, so as not to create a sense of separation from the rest of the school. In a school with falling rolls, it may be possible to allocate suitably located surplus accommodation for this purpose. In a JMI, a location between the infant and junior areas would be ideal, but if these are by nature of the existing buildings quite far apart or on different floors a possible solution would be to site support areas for infants or juniors near to their peer groups, and to provide a centrally located administrative resource near other staff areas or a library area. Examples of suitable locations are suggested in Figure 11.

Educational needs – secondary level

4.18   The degree to which special provision needs to be incorporated in a secondary school will depend to some extent on what range of curriculum and teaching methods are already offered in the school (see paragraphs 7.23–28). The numbers present who have moderate learning difficulties and the degree of their difficulty will also have an effect.

4.19   Pupils with moderate learning difficulties registered in a mainstream class of their year group (usually one or two in each) may follow an individual timetable similar in part to that of their peers but including time spent in a support space with special needs teachers and/or learning material tailored to their needs. They may also need special equipment in order to progress at their own pace. The support space is also a resource of material and special expertise which can be drawn on by the mainstream teacher.

4.20   Those pupils whose needs are more complex may in their first year or two have to spend a considerable proportion of their time in a support centre, many gradually increasing their time in mainstream classes or sets to the majority of their time. For some who have difficulty with many aspects of the curriculum, activities in the support centre may also include work in practical subjects.

4.21   A leavers' centre may provide additional support in developing life skills for these pupils, as well as serving others in the school. The support provided might include work experience sessions or link courses with further education colleges.

Accommodation requirements – secondary level

General school provision

4.22   Ideally, the range of spaces provided for subjects or activities should have sufficient variety in size and degree of specialisation, to accommodate a curriculum which embraces the needs of pupils with moderate learning difficulties. A school where the majority of classrooms are squarish, 45–54m² without sinks, and where all specialist and practical spaces are heavily equipped each for a particular subject, is unlikely to be flexible enough for a curriculum suitable for the less able as this may involve a much closer relationship between practical and non-practical work. (See also paragraphs 7.24–25.)

Support space

4.23   Requirements include

- preparation space
- space for individual work
- provision for group support work.

The first two will be required if sufficient space is not already available in the school. Provision for group support work could include any of the following, depending on numbers and degree of need:

- For one group of several pupils who need to be with a special teacher for part of their time, a *support classroom* with sink should be provided, with an adjoining resources store for work and resource material, several study carrels, and scope for using individual audiovisual aids.

Secondary pupil using special resources and equipment in an individual study carrel

- If a large school is divided into separate upper and lower schools, *one such support area or classroom in each main part of the school* might be needed, involving two to four teachers.

- Where provision is required for a large number and to supplement existing accommodation, a group of spaces forming a *support centre* would be appropriate, for use by three to six teachers.

- For those pupils for whom it would be appropriate, a *leavers' centre* could be provided, with, if feasible, a nearby small flat or other dwelling.

4.24   Where more than one support classroom is provided, a small office would be needed for the co-ordinating teacher, who may also be co-ordinating the teaching of a large number of the less able children in the school.

4.25   If a support centre were provided, it would be designed to support the curriculum of pupils with moderate learning difficulties for a proportion of their time and additionally for groups of pupils with milder learning difficulties. It would be able to offer a wider range of facilities than a support classroom.

4.26   Examples of support classrooms and centres will be found in Figures 18, 23 and 24; a leavers' centre is illustrated in Figure 22.

Location of support spaces

4.27   As in primary schools, the aim is to make support spaces integral to the rest of the school, although a leavers' centre may be detached from the main school building.

Children with sensory handicaps

4.28   Children with hearing impairment or visual handicap have been grouped together in this section, as their accommodation needs are similar, although they would not be taught together in the same support group. They can be encouraged to make use of their residual sense with suitable aids and equipment and appropriate teaching. In some cases it will be necessary to make use of other sensory channels. Some children with sensory handicaps may have additional difficulties, such as physical disability, moderate learning difficulty or emotional and behavioural problems. No attempt has been made here to give the requirements for the different vision defects.

4.29   In order for these children to be educated in ordinary schools, a well designed environment is required, so that the effect of the child's disabilities is minimised and special aids can be used to maximum benefit. The requirements of the physical environment are described in paragraphs 4.38–43.

Educational needs

4.30   The range of support which may be needed includes special aids and equipment, and suitable teaching resources. Support from a specialist teacher (or welfare assistant) within the ordinary class may sometimes be required, as well as general support from a peripatetic service.

4.31   Pupils may spend part of their time out of the ordinary class for specialised tutorial and general reinforcement, speech and communication work, language training, reading, teaching of braille, typing etc and mobility training, and also in some cases for special group teaching. Secretarial and ancillary support (audiotaping, brailling, typing, copying, retrieval) may be needed, especially in a secondary school.

Accommodation requirements

4.32   Broadly, the requirements are the same for primary and secondary levels.

General school provision

4.33   In addition to the range of accommodation to

9

be found in well-designed primary and secondary schools, space should be allowed in teaching areas to enable a pupil to be seated so as to see the teacher clearly and to select the most appropriate position for different tasks, and for an additional adult when required.

Infants' small tutorial group

Support spaces

4.34   One or more of the following may be required:

- provision for the storage of aids and equipment, and facilities for hearing aid battery charging
- area for preparing additional special teaching resources
- small room for withdrawal for one-to-one or small group work, and speech training
- in a secondary school, a suitably equipped individual study area, if there is not adequate provision in the school.

4.35   In addition, for pupils who require more support and who are likely to be brought together as a group for part of the time, a special support area or centre will be required. This will comprise all the items listed above, and in primary schools will also include:

- a teaching area for each group of up to eight, comprising general teaching area and practical facilities in or adjacent to it
- small quiet bay or room attached to the general teaching area.

In secondary schools, it will also include:

- one or more general teaching areas for groups of up to eight, preferably with sink and worktop or practical bay
- individual study area.

In all cases, sufficient socket outlets should be provided.

4.36   Suitable support spaces are illustrated in Figures 9 and 10 (primary schools), and Figures 19, 20 and 25 (secondary schools).

Location of support area or centre

4.37   Wherever possible the support area or centre should be accommodated centrally, and not physically isolated from the main body of the school. Where new building can only take place on the periphery of the school, it is preferable for the support space to be housed in existing accommodation and for the new building to be used for those activities which have been displaced.

Physical environment

4.38   The physical environment of the whole school in which hearing impaired or visually handicapped pupils are present should meet the standards specified in Design Note 17.[1] Where necessary, accommodation should be upgraded to meet these requirements.

4.39   In the design of support spaces, the recommendations given in Design Note 25[2] should be followed. Apart from detailed information on lighting and acoustics, Design Note 25 contains general guidance on the design of spaces for these two groups, and should be read in conjunction with this document. Particular reference should be made to the checklists for adaptations to existing schools.

4.40   The aim should be to provide for these children only in those schools which meet these standards or can be modified to do so. Many older schools, for instance, have hard floors, walls and ceilings, with few absorbent surfaces, and unless these can be acoustically treated many hearing impaired children may turn their aids off when conditions are particularly uncomfortable. Some of the most important provisions (given in more detail in Design Note 25) are as follows.

4.41   For both groups, good natural and artificial lighting are required in all teaching situations, with areas of lower illumination for certain children who need it. Adequate glare control is essential. Similarly for both groups attention should be paid to satisfactory acoustic conditions and adequate sound attenuation between spaces in support areas.

4.42   For hearing impaired pupils, it should be possible in all teaching spaces to arrange for them to be seated so that light falls on the teacher's face to

1.   *Guidelines for Environmental Design and Fuel Conservation in Educational Buildings.* Design Note 17, DES, 1981.

2.   *Lighting and Acoustic Criteria for the Visually Handicapped and Hearing Impaired in Schools.* Design Note 25, DES, 1981.

facilitate lip-reading, and with an unobstructed view of chalkboard or screen. The use of radio aids obviates the need for these pupils to be seated immediately in front of the teacher. In practical areas, an adequate visual warning system must be fitted, particularly where noisy activities such as woodwork are taking place. When OHP and other visual aids are used for which blackout is usually provided, it is helpful if local lighting is provided on the teacher's face; alternatively, dimout rather than blackout can be used so that the pupil can still see the teacher speaking.

4.43 Some visually handicapped pupils may require adjustable local lighting, particularly in science bases or for complex tasks in other areas. Colour can be used to differentiate work surfaces and pieces of equipment, in the home studies area for example. Main routes can be colour coded, and changes in level and other hazards identified with changes in colour and texture. Fire escape routes should be clearly defined.

Children with speech and language disorders

Educational needs

4.44 A child suffering from delayed language development, severe problems of articulation, or other difficulties in communicating, may otherwise have a wide range of intellectual functioning. These children will need clear positive direction in well-defined learning tasks, and much repetition; they may need attention training, and emphasis on visual material to supplement auditory perception.

4.45 At the stage when they require this help, usually during some part of their primary years, the children will spend most of their time in a special support group or class (generally of between six and eight children) which has a full-time teacher and support from a speech therapist, both of whom will work with individuals and small groups. There will be opportunities for the children to join in some mainstream class activities.

Accommodation requirements

4.46 The class base for each special group should include:

- general teaching area capable of rearrangement into activity areas
- a quiet bay / reading corner
- good provision for wet and messy / creative activities, desirable even for the older children in the group

- storage and display for a wide range of teaching material, aids and equipment
- facilities for using individual and group audiovisual aids
- easy access to outdoor work area and adequate grassed play area
- readily available area for dance, drama, music and movement, and imaginative play, to encourage self expression – unless a suitable uncommitted floor space is readily available elsewhere in the school
- a room for speech therapy, separate from the class base but preferably adjacent to it, and capable of accommodating two or three pupils (though it will normally be used on a one-to-one basis). A full-length mirror, natural lighting and acoustic treatment to walls are needed.

A suitable area is illustrated in Figure 12.

Location of class base

4.47 A ground floor location with access to outdoor play areas is particularly desirable. If the classroom is for infants it should preferably be near other infant classrooms; if provision is made for infants and juniors the support areas should be close to each other and ideally lie between infant and junior parts of the school.

Children with emotional and behavioural disorders

Educational needs

4.48 The curriculum needs of pupils whose main difficulties are emotional and behavioural disturbance will cover a wide range; there may be associated mild or moderate learning difficulty, and sometimes also mild physical or sensory disabilities. At present, larger numbers of children are identified as having emotional and behavioural disorders at secondary than at primary level.

4.49 These children will divide their time, according to their needs, between working in mainstream classes (perhaps with support from a special needs teacher); working individually or in small groups with a special needs teacher; and working in a special group. Some who experience only temporary difficulties may spend most of their time in the mainstream class and only occasionally need to work in a special support centre; others who undergo a longer or more severe period of disturbance may need to spend all or most of their time in a specially equipped centre, which will need to cater for most of their curriculum needs. The time spent in support provision may gradually decrease, but these children will still need access to a special teacher at times for counselling, encouragement and help when they require it.

4.50   These children may have a particular need to be able to work with a minimum of disturbance from the proximity of other children or from circulatory movement. They will need plenty of scope for quiet activities in a private environment and practical work, whether in the mainstream class or in a support group.

Accommodation requirements — primary level

Ordinary class bases

4.51   These will be most supportive if they have the facilities found in a good modern primary school (see paragraphs 6.42–43). In addition it is essential that the disturbed pupil should have plenty of space to work without undue pressures from other pupils.

Support space

4.52   The range includes:

- *small group room or quiet rooms,* close to the ordinary teaching base, for teaching individuals or small groups and providing a quiet environment (see Figures 5 and 6)
- for a larger group of pupils, a *support area.*

4.53   A group support area for younger children is more likely to be needed at junior level, and in a small to medium primary school only one such area is likely to be required. It would comprise a self-contained classroom containing provision for practical work and with:

- small enclosed room opening off the classroom
- storage space.

A suitable area is illustrated in Figure 13.

Location of support area

4.54   A support area at primary level should ideally be an integral part of the main school building, convenient to other teaching areas and communal spaces. However, there should be a degree of seclusion: the class and its immediate outside area should not be overlooked, nor its activities subject to interruption by circulation or extraneous noise.

Accommodation requirements — secondary level

General school provision

4.55   As at primary level, there should be sufficient space in the mainstream class for a pupil to work with minimal disturbance.

Support space

4.56   The range includes:

- a small study space or tutorial room, which should be available for individual or small group extraction from the ordinary class, and equipped for individual study
- a one-teacher support classroom for eight to ten pupils
- a two-teacher support centre for about 16 pupils.

One-teacher support classroom

4.57   A suitable classroom is illustrated in Figure 21. It should consist of:

- a general teaching area with sink and worktop
- area for individual work
- small group room for withdrawal
- lockable storage.

The room provides mainly for back-up work, as it is assumed that specialist subject work for these pupils will largely be conducted in mainstream classes. If some pupils in the group need simple practical facilities, or perhaps to spend more time on a particular piece of work than would be possible in the main school accommodation, they might use the facilities provided in a larger centre for pupils with moderate learning difficulties, if time and space were available.

4.58   This support classroom should be in a fairly central position, within reasonable reach of the other teaching spaces these pupils will be using.

Two-teacher support centre

4.59   This type of centre is suitable for those needing to spend most of their time out of mainstream classes. It will therefore need to have a wide range of facilities covering most of the curriculum, and should comprise:

- a classroom with sink
- small group room
- a quiet/discussion or social/noisy room with soft finishes
- a small enclosed craft support room

- small kitchen/home studies bay, perhaps linked to
- social/study area.

A suitable centre is illustrated in Figure 26.

4.60   The centre should be within the school building although its indoor and outdoor activities should not be overlooked by other teaching or outdoor areas.

4.61   External facilities for these pupils could include rural or environmental studies, perhaps sharing in what is generally available, and also some covered hard surface area for craft or mechanical projects.

Children with physical disabilities

Educational needs

4.62   Children with physical disabilities may be catered for in an ordinary school if it has an appropriate curriculum and a supportive organisation. They may cover the whole ability range, and many will be following all or most of the normal curriculum, with or without special equipment or teaching aids. Some may need occasional periods of smaller group or individual teaching, while others may have special educational needs similar to those with moderate learning difficulties.

4.63   In addition to the appropriate curriculum, pupils may be supported in the ordinary school by any of the following:

- mobility aids, such as walking aids, wheelchairs
- physical aids, eg special typewriters
- specialist teaching equipment and/or material
- appropriate furniture
- assistance from non-teaching aides
- care and treatment facilities.

Accommodation requirements

Overall school organisation

4.64   The design studies in Chapters 5–7 are based on the assumption that, in any one school at one time, the numbers of physically disabled pupils using wheelchairs will be small – there might be two or three in a small primary school, for example, and between three and 12 in an average size secondary school. Exceptionally, the numbers will be greater and in such cases the scale of ancillary provision and circulation space will need special consideration. The small numbers usually make it possible to accommodate these children without organisational

difficulties. For instance, in a primary school it will not generally be necessary to accommodate more than one child in a wheelchair in a practical area at any one time, and a situation where there might be more than one can be avoided by a suitable arrangement of classes.

4.65   In a secondary school, forward planning is particularly important to ensure access for pupils in wheelchairs to specialist and other spaces according to their chosen curriculum. With suitable timetabling, it may be possible to meet their educational requirements without making alterations to buildings, if the areas to which they require access are on the ground floor and if there is adequate circulation space. However, in many schools access to the upper floors will be necessary: an example of a two-storey secondary school which has been adapted to provide access for the physically disabled to all spaces is given in Figure 30.

Access to site and buildings

4.66   The basic provision set out in Design Note 18[1] is essential, but subject to the numbers of physically disabled pupils in the school this provision may need to be augmented.

Access to the learning environment

4.67   The requirements include:

- sufficient space within teaching areas to allow access for a pupil in a wheelchair or using walking aids to all the main teaching activities (see paragraph 4.69)
- consideration of furniture layouts and choice of appropriate furniture to make classroom management easier
- sufficient space for an additional adult to work in an area when required
- suitable working surfaces and heights (see paragraphs 4.70–71)
- adequate electrical services for special teaching aids, within easy reach of the pupil
- space for parking wheelchairs.

4.68   In practical subject areas, layout and suitable working heights are critical, and consideration should also be given to:

- the provision of service outlets (gas, water, electricity) within easy reach
- access to storage for protective clothing

---

1.   *Access for the Physically Disabled to Educational Buildings.* Design Note 18, DES, 1979. (Revised edition in preparation.)

- ready access to handwashing facilities when using paints, varnishes, etc, for pupils with poor hand coordination.

Examples of suitable adaptations of practical and other common teaching areas are given in Figures 16 and 29. Some work space requirements are shown in the Appendix, Figure A6.

This science laboratory allows adequate passing widths for a secondary pupil with walking aids

Layout of spaces

4.69   To allow adequate passing widths for pupils using wheelchairs or other walking aids, a minimum clear width of 800mm between loose furniture, and 1000mm in front of fixed furniture, is required (see Figures A6 and A7). Where furniture is mostly fixed or retained in one layout, circulation routes may be established and maintained more easily. In rooms with long rows of worktops or tables and seating, a minimum passing width of 900mm is preferred. Where unobstructed turning space is needed for a wheelchair, a useful check is to draw a circle on the room layout plan of 1500–1700mm diameter.

Work surfaces and heights

4.70   The wide variation in physical needs and abilities relating to standing, sitting, reaching etc precludes any standardisation of requirements for all pupils with physical disabilities for all types of activity. Reference should always be made to the pupils' paramedical advisers when determining whether modifications are required to existing fitted work surfaces to achieve a correct working position for a particular activity. They will also give advice on any particular requirements and may suggest some simple modifications, such as the addition of retaining edges on work surfaces, or pull-out flaps below standard worktops with wells to hold mixing bowls etc, or the use of a lap tray secured to the wheelchair when a pupil is unable to use a standard worktop. Such

modifications may obviate the need for drastic alterations. The aim should be to make possible normal arrangements for working with other pupils, for instance in pairs or small groups.

4.71   The type and specification of a pupil's wheelchair may determine whether the normal class furniture is appropriate or the existing spaces suitable. A minimum clear height of 650mm will normally be required below tables or worktops, and for some pupils or activities the wheelchair may need to be closer to the table, which necessitates a height in excess of this (see Figure A7). Younger pupils in junior wheelchairs may be comfortable with a lower clear height below tables or worktops. Use of a standard table or worktop may be possible only when a wheelchair has removable armrests or is fitted with desk armrests.

4.72   Access may also be required to and within any of the following teaching spaces which are to be used for support work:

- small group, quiet or tutorial rooms

Secondary tutorial group including pupil in a wheelchair

- school resources centre or special study area
- support classroom or centre (see Figures 6b, 7, 8, 18, 23, 24 and 27).

Preparation and storage

4.73   Spaces required will include:

- easily accessible storage for mobility aids and other accessories, which could be combined with preparation space for minor adaptations to special equipment and aids (see Figure A4)
- storage for wheelchairs, with provision for chair-battery charging, where electrically powered chairs can be left overnight or at weekends (see Figure A5). Wherever provision is being made for battery charging the advice of the Fire Prevention Officer should be sought.

Care and treatment facilities

4.74   Accommodation should include:

■ suitably located, accessible WC provision (see below)

■ provision for showering and changing younger pupils, and facilities for older pupils to attend to their hygiene needs, whether independently or with assistance. This provision may or may not be associated with a suitable WC compartment

■ suitable areas for speech therapy, physiotherapy, etc (see Chapter 8)

■ availability of room for medical inspection, treatment and rest (see Chapter 8).

4.75   In nursery schools, the lavatory, bathing and changing facilities usually provided should suffice (see Figure A1). However, in primary and secondary schools, lavatory provision additional to that set out in Design Note 18 may be necessary, depending on the numbers of physically disabled pupils in the school.

4.76   For physically disabled pupils who are not wholly dependent on wheelchairs for mobility, a normal WC cubicle may be accessible provided the wheelchair can be parked nearby. Similarly for some boys the urinal provision will also be accessible, although the provision of support rails should be considered.

4.77   For pupils who require access in wheelchairs to a WC, a centrally located compartment should be provided which meets the minimum dimensional criteria set out in Design Note 18. In addition to this, a similar compartment might also be included with other pupils' WCs (see Figure A2).

5. Nursery Accommodation

General features

5.1 Well designed ordinary nursery accommodation which contains the desirable features outlined in a number of DES publications,[1] can cater for children with special educational needs. These features include:

- a range of spaces within the playroom for different activities, eg noisy, wet and messy, creative and imaginative play
- a quiet room
- access to a veranda and a nursery garden
- satisfactory storage and ancillary provision.

5.2 Children with special needs who require regular support on a one-to-one basis are likely to occupy the quiet room for longer periods on average than other children. The quiet room becomes an essential feature for withdrawal, assessment, speech work and/or training in communication skills, in addition to its usual functions as a group story room and enclosed soft furnished area. This, in addition to the increase in staff generally in the playroom and the fact that extra space will be needed for storage and use of specialist aids and equipment, increases the space requirements of a nursery, and reduces the number of children it can accommodate.

5.3 Physically disabled children require space for:

- floor-based movement – crawling and exercising – which may involve a physiotherapist in the playroom
- changing into calipers etc, either on a bench or more usually on the playroom floor
- wheelchair movement around the playroom, space for learning how to operate the chair, and for parking when the chair is not in use
- purpose-designed items of furniture, such as a strap-in, cut-out table or a standing support for work at an easel or water trolley.

Some of these items plus calipers and wheelchairs may need to be stored in a suitable place in the nursery when not in use.

Internal environment

5.4 For pupils with sensory handicaps it is essential that lighting and listening conditions throughout the nursery should be satisfactory. Good natural lighting may need to be supplemented by artificial lighting, preferably of a domestic nature, and particular attention should be paid to achieving good acoustic conditions within the quiet room and any other space used for speech and communication work and language training. For all children with special needs, the recommended provision of non-woven carpet and other resilient floor finishes to reduce impact noise at floor level, and of an acoustically absorbent ceiling, are helpful, and are even more desirable where hearing impaired children are present.

5.5 The heating and ventilation requirements appropriate for nursery schools are described in Design Note 17,[2] and should be followed wherever children with disabilities are being admitted. One important requirement is to protect children from direct contact with accessible metallic surfaces likely to have a temperature greater than 43°C. Where physically disabled pupils are present, soft floor finishes should be easy to clean as there will often be soiling.

External areas

5.6 External areas should be seen as an extension to the playroom. A well designed nursery garden which provides a rich and varied range of experience for all children[3] will be of particular benefit in the educational development of children with special needs. Easy access to an outdoor veranda is required, and a large store for indoor/outdoor play apparatus should be provided.

5.7 For physically disabled pupils access should be provided to as many features such as play mounds and slides as possible. Where there are a number of pupils dependent upon wheelchairs the hard-paved area provided should be above the minimum required by the Regulations.[4] Where children with communication difficulties or emotional problems are present, an adequate grassed area is particularly important; this should be no less than the normal minimum.

---

1. See *Building for Nursery Education* (Design Note 1, DES, 1968); *Nursery Education: Low cost adaptation of spare space in primary schools* (Broadsheet 1, DES, 1980); *Nursery Education in Converted Space* (Building Bulletin 56, HMSO, 1978).

2. *Guidelines for Environmental Design and Fuel Conservation in Educational Buildings*. Design Note 17, DES, 1981.

3. *Building for Nursery Education*. Design Note 1, DES, 1968.

4. *The Education (School Premises) Regulations 1981*. SI No 909, HMSO, 1981.

Design studies

A nursery class in a primary school

5.8   The example in Figure 1 has many of the desirable features outlined previously which make it suitable for children with special needs within the ordinary nursery class.

5.9   The nursery is provided with a range of clearly identified spaces, and the playroom can be divided by low screens into smaller areas for particular activities. There is easy access to the outdoor covered veranda, and a large store for indoor/outdoor play apparatus. In the WC area is the required deep sink, with a hand-shower; a fold-down changing bench adjacent to it would be needed for some children with physical disabilities.

5.10   The quiet room is placed away from the noisier activities and does not overlook the covered outdoor play area. It is suitable for individual or small group work without distractions and could be used for language training or for speech therapy. A well-fitting door with a gasket would improve sound insulation between the quiet room and play area, and could be glazed for ease of supervision. (Glazed panels can be fitted with blinds or curtains to avoid distraction when children are being helped on a one-to-one basis.) The quiet room is carpeted and has an acoustic ceiling. For hearing impaired pupils the addition of acoustic wall treatment would improve the listening conditions.

5.11   The nursery has windows on three sides providing good lighting for each of the activity areas, which makes it particularly suitable for partially sighted children who depend on a well lit environment. The simple layout, with quieter zones on one side and lack of obstruction in the play area, would enable visually handicapped children to move around with relative ease. Visual clues such as a low-level dado in contrasting colour would help them find their way for example to the wet play sink and the lavatories.

Figure 1.   A nursery class in a primary school

Outdoor play equipment adapted for physically disabled children

A nursery school/centre

5.12   The school shown in Figure 2 has playroom capacity for up to 60 nursery children. These might form three groups for which there is one self-contained playroom with its own quiet room, and a larger area where two groups would each have a home area; there is an enclosed story/quiet room, a quiet bay, an area for wet and messy activities and a space that can be cleared for musical activities. The two playroom areas are separated by only one door so that movement between them is easy.

5.13   One or two children with special needs might be present in any of these groups, in which case there may be additional adult help, or peripatetic paramedical staff. The quiet rooms may be more in demand therefore for one-to-one or small group work. If five or six children with special needs are present, they might form part of a smaller teaching group of, say, ten to twelve in the self-contained playroom. Intensive use can be made of the quiet room for one-to-one or small group work as well as for stories for the whole group. Whichever arrangement is adopted, the total capacity of the nursery is reduced.

5.14   The lavatories are easily reached by a child with a physical disability and there is a raised shower tray, hand-shower and fold-down changing table for dealing adequately with any child's 'accidents'.

5.15   If it were considered desirable to have a small nursery class, for example for hearing impaired children, serving a wide catchment area, it could be accommodated for part of the time in the smaller, separate playroom. The whole nursery may then be used by all the children on a general basis, but for more concentrated teaching in quiet conditions the hearing impaired group could be withdrawn to this space.

5.16   The nursery is well lit and provides an interesting variety of spaces. The smaller scale and simpler layout of the enclosed group area would make it suitable for either an individual child or a small group of children with visual handicap, particularly as a first introduction to the school. They could move into the other areas as they became more confident.

5.17   The provision for staff and parents includes a head's room or office for discussion or interview; a

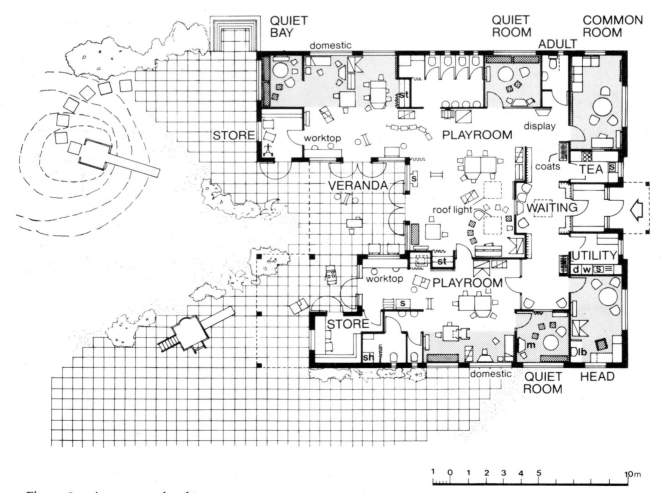

Figure 2.   A nursery school/centre

commonroom for staff, students or parents to relax or work in; a central space for parents to arrive with children; and a small separate tea and hot drink preparation area which can be used by parents when the staff room is in use. The adult WC is suitable for wheelchair access. All of these features are supportive to staff and parents working with children with special needs in the nursery school.

A nursery/infant school with a family centre

5.18   Figure 3 illustrates a nursery/infant school, which was designed[1] to facilitate a variety of forms of organisation and which provides a suitable range of spaces for small group and individual work and for general teaching. The school is well treated acoustically with mineral ceiling tiles, curtains and carpeted areas, which would reduce sound disturbance in this comparatively open design.

5.19   An interesting feature of this school, which would make it particularly suitable for accommodating individual children with special needs, is its family centre. This provides rooms for discussion and coffee and social activities, adjacent to

staff/adult facilities. The centre could form the base for a pre-school link for children with special needs, and throughout the child's time at the school the parents can be encouraged to play an active role in helping the child's development. The plan illustrates the family centre,[2] and the nursery and transition classes. Some additional washing facilities might be needed, as illustrated in Figure A1.

---

1.   *Chaucer Infant and Nursery School, Ilkeston, Derbyshire.* Design Note 11, DES, 1973.

2.   This is described in more detail in *Community Use of Primary Schools,* Broadsheet 15, DES, 1983.

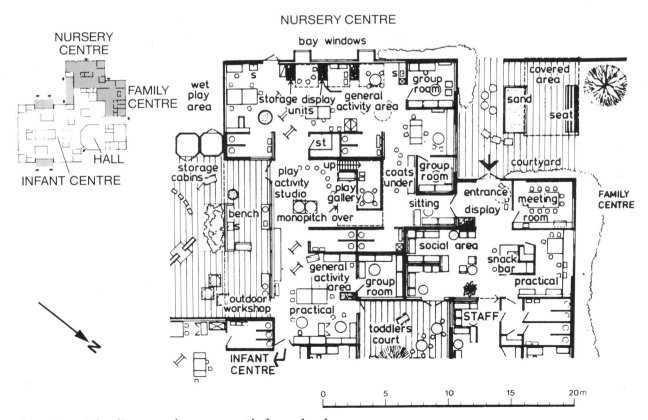

Figure 3.   **A family centre in a nursery/infant school**

6. Primary School Accommodation

Design studies: examples of support spaces

6.1 The following examples illustrate how the types of support space listed in Chapter 4 might be provided. They are designed to cover the range of circumstances that might arise.

Preparation room

6.2 The room in Figure 4 provides for the preparation and storage of specific teaching materials and storage of teaching aids and equipment. It will be necessary when children with special educational needs are supported in mainstream classes and when no special teaching support space is provided, if there is insufficient preparation and storage space available for these purposes in the school. The preparation room, though it is not intended for teaching, could be close to a small withdrawal room as a combined support provision for a number of individual children with special needs.

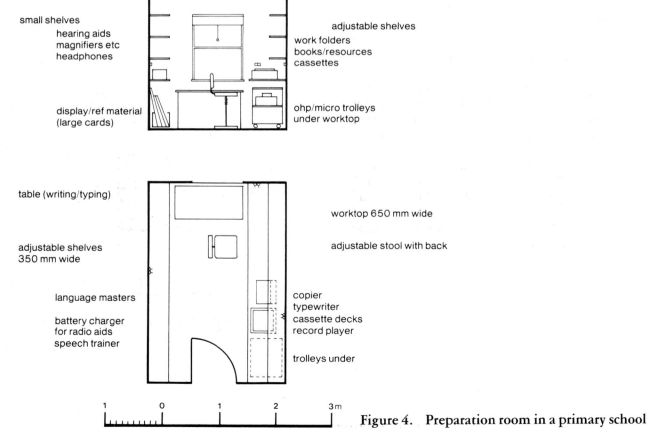

Figure 4. Preparation room in a primary school

6.3   In the example shown a hardboard or melamine-topped worktop/shelf is provided at adult working height along one side for cutting out, gluing, covering etc and for storage of some larger items of recording or playing equipment. Adjustable shelves are fitted above for resource material, box files, cartons etc; space under the worktop can accommodate OHP or audiovisual trolleys, display material, mobile material bins etc. Along the other long side a shelf at adult work height is wide enough for the smaller individual reading and language aids, headphones etc, with adjustable shelves above. A microcomputer for specialised teaching programs might be kept here, if not available elsewhere. A table and chair may be useful if the room is to be used for writing or typing.

6.4   Additional storage requirements might be:

- *for hearing impaired pupils:* radio aids and battery charger, spare leads, batteries and receivers, various kinds of hearing aid, speech trainer, language training equipment.
- *for visually handicapped pupils:* large print typewriter, large print books and resources, magnifiers and other low vision aids, brailling equipment and resources, closed-circuit television and computer accessories.

6.5   The preparation room should be ventilated and suitably lit for the range of tasks described. At least three double socket outlets are needed for use at worktop level. It should not be encumbered with heating or electrical apparatus serving other parts of the school.

Small quiet/tutorial room

6.6   Figure 5 shows a room intended for working with one–three children with special needs at a time which is an essential provision in a primary school where suitable accommodation is not available. It could also be used for a pupil to work quietly on his or her own or for withdrawal of a disturbed child, and would be available for use by peripatetic teachers and other visiting specialists. It might be close to a small preparation space. The room should be approximately 7.5m² in area, and provided with soft furniture and a carpet as shown.

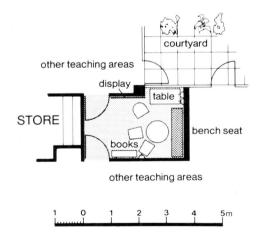

Figure 5.   Small tutorial/quiet room in a primary school

Small group rooms

6.7   Figure 6a shows a small group room of approximately 15m² plus storage, equipped for the use of a variety of learning aids, for both group and individual study. Rooms of this size are often provided in primary schools close to class bases for stories and small group work: this one is centrally located in the school, and is set aside for a particular range of activities. Children may use this space for short bursts of support work using teaching aids and special teaching materials. It would mainly be used by children with mild or moderate learning difficulties (see paragraph 4.13) in small groups, but would also be suitable where two or three hearing impaired children are receiving peripatetic teaching.

6.8   A teacher or peripatetic teacher may work here with up to three or four pupils at a time, while three other children may at the same time be using the study booths (carrels),equipped with socket outlets, for individual learning. Pin-up board and shelves facilitate the display of material and books, and lockable storage is available for audiovisual aids. In this example of a room in an existing school, the study/resource room is immediately adjacent to the school's central library area and is available to other pupils at times for quiet study.

6.9   Figure 6b shows a larger room of 20m² plus storage, which allows for a group of six–eight pupils and teacher, with more space for access to learning material and use of audiovisual aids on a trolley. The carrels are 900mm wide to allow the use of several pieces of equipment together and also a small desktop microcomputer. If one of these pupils is in a wheelchair, the area will permit movement around the room with six pupils around a central table.

Figure 6.   Small group rooms in a primary school

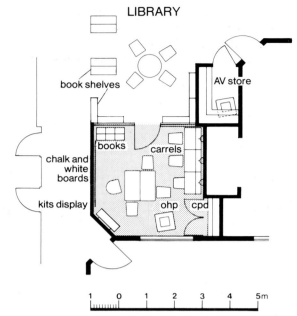

Figure 6a

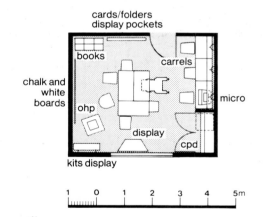

Figure 6b

6.10 Two design studies are illustrated, one (in Figure 7) for the conversion of three existing classrooms in an older primary school and the second (Figure 8) as part of a new school design. Both of the support centres offer work places for up to 20 pupils with moderate learning difficulties aged 5–11 in two groups: the younger group might have between eight and ten pupils, the older between ten and twelve. As numbers in an age range may change from year to year, the spaces provide for the larger number in each case. (See also paragraph 4.15.)

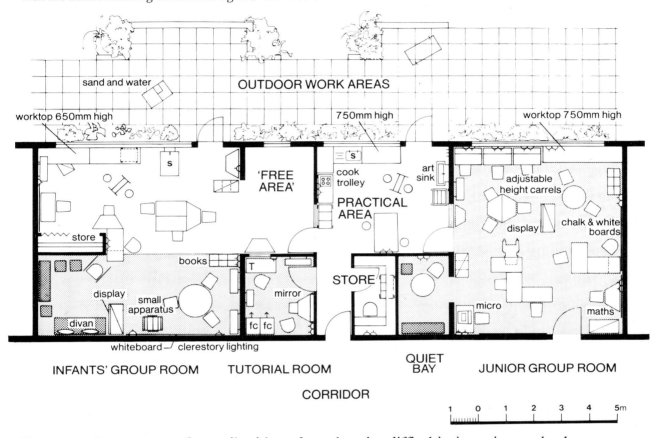

Figure 7a. Support centre for pupils with moderate learning difficulties in a primary school

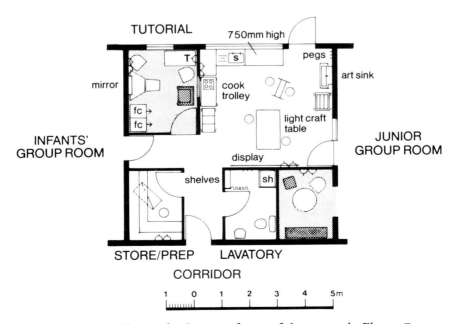

Figure 7b. Alternative layout of part of the centre in Figure 7a

6.11   In Figure 7a, the existing rooms, two of approximately 53m² and one of 43m², are located in the body of the school, all opening off a central circulation route. The remodelled accommodation comprises two separate group rooms, a practical area, a tutorial room/office and a store.

6.12   For the younger group, an easily supervised space is provided where the full range of learning activities for 5–7 year old children can take place. Part of the area is carpeted for small group teaching and a book corner, and a semi-enclosed story/quiet bay opens off this. In the remaining space, painting and modelling, some sand and water play and 3D play-learning activities are provided for. A full-height storage bay is needed for small and large boxes of learning apparatus, kits, paper etc.

6.13   For the older group, there is a self-contained carpeted classroom for bookwork, mathematics, etc. Three individual work carrels are included where individual teaching aids such as language masters can be plugged in and used without distraction. To enable individual work on a microcomputer, a suitable corner away from the window is supplied with double electric socket outlets. A small semi-enclosed bay for stories, one-to-one work or quiet group work opens off the classroom for easy supervision by the teacher. A glazed panel and door link the classroom with a small practical area which can also be used by a separate small group of juniors.

6.14   When the older pupils who normally receive support are elsewhere, the teaching space can be used by a group of up to 15 other pupils in the school with their teacher for setting or remedial support.

6.15   Between the two group teaching areas, a small 'office' is available for staff to keep records and have discussions with staff, parents, visiting paramedical staff and therapists, and where adults may also work with individual pupils. Specific material or equipment for one-to-one work will be kept either here or in a nearby lockable store. A glazed panel allows staff to oversee adjoining areas.

6.16   The centre's main store may house all vulnerable equipment (audiovisual aids etc). A worktop is provided for preparation of material and adjustment of equipment. A service trolley and/or OHP trolley may be stored here.

6.17   There is direct access from the support centre to an external paved area for outdoor work and play.

6.18   As space is available, a small 'uncommitted' floor area has been provided, which can be rearranged by staff for a variety of educational and therapeutic activities. For one term it could house several small or one large container for water play, for another it might have a large foam shape, and for another it could be carpeted and form an imaginative hideout

area. Other pupils in the school might also be able to share this facility.

6.19   Where existing lavatories are some distance away from the centre it will be helpful to add a small unit containing one WC, one lavatory basin, a low shower tray or Belfast sink and a hand-shower. This unit, which would be primarily used by younger children and on occasion by an older child, is illustrated in the alternative layout in Figure 7b, which makes use of the 'uncommitted' area described above.

6.20   Where there is a shortage of indoor lavatories in an existing school, or if the whole school is designed with a few WCs etc close to each single or paired classroom, the appropriate number of sanitary fittings for this centre would be a minimum of one WC and one lavatory basin for girls and one WC, one urinal and two lavatory basins for boys, with a separate small shower space to be used by either.

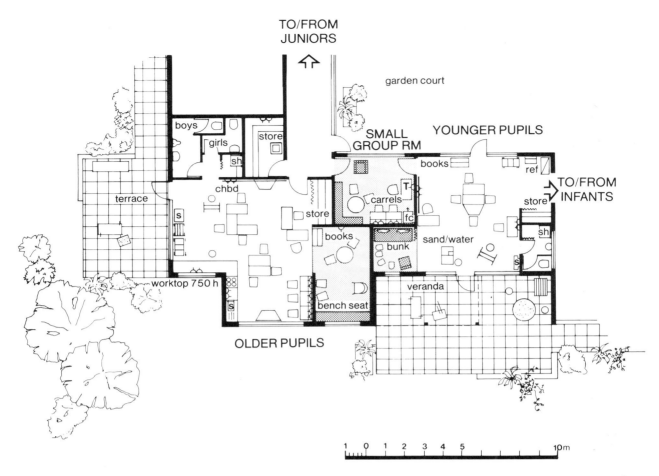

Figure 8.   Support centre for pupils with moderate learning difficulties in a primary school

6.21   The support centre illustrated in Figure 8 is shown as part of a new school design, but the ingredients could be adopted for conversion. The accommodation comprises two separate group rooms each with practical facilities, access to an outdoor area and lavatories. There is an enclosed room between the bases for small group and one-to-one teaching and office use, and a lockable store.

6.22   The support area for the younger pupils has a small carpeted bay for retreat, story or occasional rest, but otherwise a homogeneous resilient floor surface. The support area for the older pupils has a large carpeted semi-enclosed bay for quieter work and group listening, and the remaining area can be sub-divided with furniture for general learning and practical activities.

Support centre for hearing impaired pupils

6.23 The design study shown in Figure 9 is for the conversion of three existing classrooms in a primary school to form a support centre for up to 14 pupils with hearing impairment aged 5–11 years (see paragraphs 4.34–35).

6.24 Three classrooms (two of 53m² and one of 43m²), all located off a corridor between infant and junior areas in the school, have been modified to form separate support areas for younger and older pupils, a shared tutorial room/office, and a store. Part of the existing area was combined with the corridor to create a library/study area as a common resource for the whole school.

6.25 The infant area is designed to be easily supervised by one adult (although others may sometimes be present) and is equipped to support a wide range of activities. It incorporates a quiet corner for reading, an area for painting, modelling, and sand and water play, and a general learning area. The room is carpeted to increase sound absorption and reduce disturbance from furniture and trolleys, except for the area for wet and messy activities where the flooring would be foam-backed vinyl. Provision

includes a worktop and sinks. There is direct access to an outside play area.

6.26 In the illustration tables and chairs are shown in a semi-circle facing the teacher for language and communication work, for example, with the aid of an overhead projector. The furniture used could also be laid out informally for individual and small group work. Equally, tables could be moved aside for children to be gathered in a small circle around the teacher, or to create space for floor-based activities.

6.27 The junior area includes a carpeted general teaching space for group work in a range of basic subjects as well as specific support in language and communication, a practical bay with external access, and a quiet bay for individual and small group work and reading. This bay is designed as a semi-open area for easy supervision but could be fitted with a door to improve sound separation if necessary. An individual pupil can work on a microcomputer or other learning apparatus in a corner of the general teaching area away from the windows to avoid reflection and glare.

6.28 The tutorial room would be available to both younger and older groups for individual withdrawal,

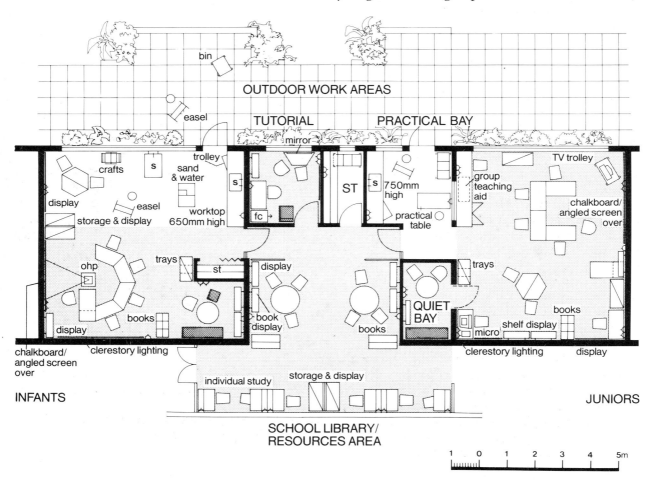

Figure 9. Support centre for hearing impaired pupils in a primary school

language training, speech work etc, as well as providing a space for staff to keep records and to talk with visiting specialists, parents and teachers from mainstream classes. An adjustable mirror fitted to a low table is shown against the window so that light is evenly distributed on the faces of child and tutor. A full length mirror may also be needed. The windows would be fitted with blinds to cut out glare.

6.29   The central lockable store would be used for shared items of equipment eg OHP, slide projector, tape recorder, television, and general teaching resources and materials, as well as a range of hearing aids, battery charger for radio aids and other specialist pieces of equipment.

6.30   The carpeted library resource area, with study bays provided, is easily accessible to all children working in that part of the school.

6.31   The teaching spaces are well lit with clerestory lighting along the corridor walls, and window wall opposite. Additional task lighting could be provided as required. Acoustic tiled ceilings and acoustic wall treatment would be used throughout to achieve a reverberation time of 0.5 seconds in the general teaching spaces and 0.4 seconds in the tutorial room. The intermediate space of the library/resource area increases the sound insulation between the support centre and the corridor. (See also paragraphs 4.38–43).

Support area for pupils with visual handicap

6.32   Figure 10 shows a room furnished and equipped for a small group of visually handicapped pupils. It has good natural lighting. A number of working spaces for individuals or small groups are arranged in well lit positions around the perimeter of the room, and a further group is located in the centre, facing chalkboard and/or screen. All would have access to individual task lighting if required. A reading corner is included with plenty of storage and display, eg for large print books and tapes, and a study space where pupils can use closed-circuit television, tape recorders, and other learning and audiovisual aids. A worktop and sink are provided. The room is well provided with storage cupboards and trolleys for a wide range of learning materials, aids and equipment. The range of specialised furniture which may need to be accommodated includes adjustable sloping tables, table top adjustable boards and reading stands, wall and table-fixed adjustable display stands, etc. The support area has immediate access to an outside paved area where pupils may work in good light. The shared quiet room next door could be used for one-to-one support and visiting specialists. (More detail on suitable internal environment will be found in paragraphs 4.38–43.)

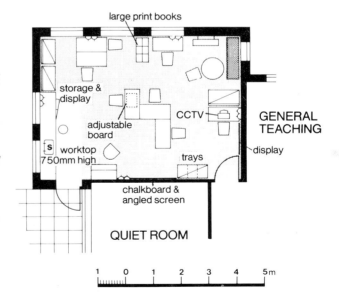

Figure 10.   Support area for pupils with visual handicap in a primary school

Location of support areas for pupils with moderate learning difficulties or sensory handicaps

6.33   Suitable locations for support centres, as described in paragraphs 4.17 and 4.37, are suggested in Figure 11, which shows a range of possible solutions in different types of existing primary schools.

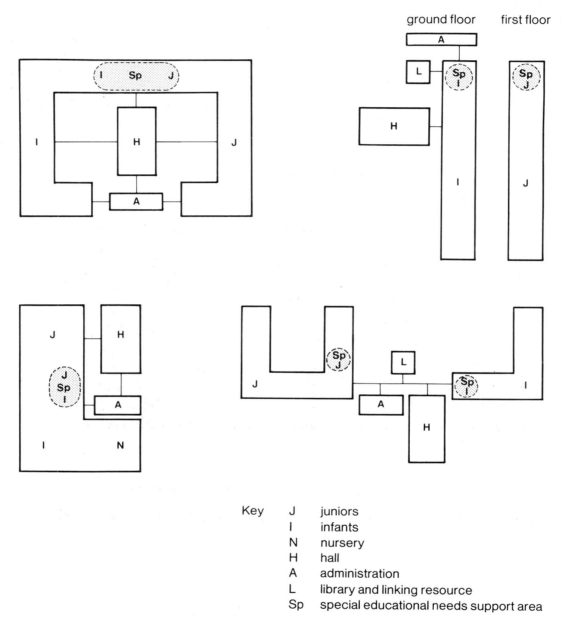

Key   J   juniors
      I   infants
      N   nursery
      H   hall
      A   administration
      L   library and linking resource
      Sp special educational needs support area

Figure 11.   Location of support areas in primary schools for pupils with moderate learning difficulties or sensory handicaps

Support area for pupils with speech and language disorders

6.34   In Figure 12, two ordinary classrooms have been converted to form a support area (as described in paragraph 4.46) for a group of six to eight pupils, mainly at the lower end of the 5–11 age range, with speech and language disorders. The design considerations apply equally to purpose-built accommodation.

6.35   The new classroom (approximately $51m^2$) is carpeted over half of the floor area, and each half can be rearranged into appropriate small areas for particular activities. Generous storage and display are provided, including a walk-in lockable store for audiovisual trolley etc. There is direct access to a variety of outside play spaces including suitable grassed area.

6.36   A tutorial room for speech therapy and one-to-one work opens off the classroom. This has natural lighting and should be acoustically treated. Storage for therapy equipment and records is provided. Adequate socket outlets are required in both rooms for tape recorders, language machines etc.

6.37   The area selected for conversion allows for a small drama/music/movement room to be provided adjacent to the group's classroom. Primarily intended as an immediately available resource to children with speech and language difficulties, it is also accessible to other classes. As this area could be a major noise source, it is not adjacent to the tutorial room described above.

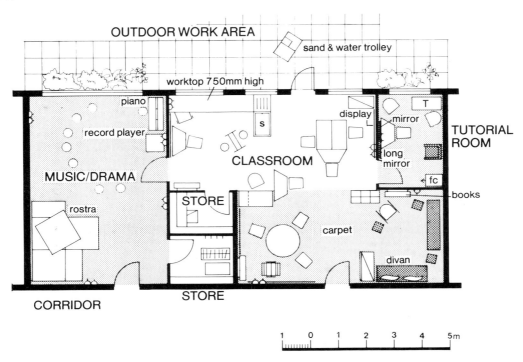

Figure 12.   Support area for pupils with speech and language disorders in a primary school

Support area for pupils with emotional and behavioural disorders

6.38   The accommodation illustrated in Figure 13 comprises an L-shaped classroom with practical facilities, a lockable store and an adjacent kiva (see paragraph 4.53). The classroom has work places for up to eight pupils; much of their work may be on an individual basis and ages and stages will vary, so there will be a considerable amount of teaching material to accommodate. The area should allow for arrangement of work tables in various ways while still providing adequate free space around each pupil. A resilient or sound-absorbing floor finish and sound absorbing ceiling are required.

6.39   With its small practical bay, this classroom is fairly self-contained but it is assumed that for some activities other facilities in the school will be used when pupils join in with other groups. A wall-mounted telephone or call buzzer should be fitted in a central location convenient to the teacher's work station, as there may at times be two adults working in the room but sometimes one only.

6.40   The adjoining kiva is similar to a quiet room of approximately 12m². At times it would be used by some of the group for imaginative games, role play, stories etc; at other times it would be needed for a child going through a period of disturbance to spend a while quietly on his or her own. The kiva should have a quiet welcoming appearance and be simply furnished preferably with fixed items. (In this example there is a built-in carpeted step seat.) Attention should be given to: the robustness of partition linings and doors; window openings designed to prevent egress; avoidance of protruding surfaces, controls or equipment if possible, and the use of safety glass in door panels and windows (normally recommended in schools for doors and lower windows). Walls should offer possibilities for display, but movable display boards or shelves would not be appropriate here.

6.41   A small room for interview or case work is required but does not need to be immediately adjacent to this support area, provided a convenient and suitable 'office' space is available when needed elsewhere in the school.

Figure 13.   Support area for pupils with emotional and behavioural disorders in a primary school

30

General supportive features of the whole primary school

6.42   In addition to the specific support spaces described above, there are certain features of the school as a whole which are particularly supportive to children with special educational needs. These may be found in many new or remodelled primary schools, and are summarised below:

(i)   a variety of sizes and types of teaching spaces

(ii)   class bases of suitable shapes which provide general teaching space capable of formal and informal layout, space for practical/creative activities, and a carpeted bay for quiet activities

(iii) small group rooms, close to class bases, for quiet work in small groups or whole class story/discussion groups

(iv)   at least one small room for individual teaching or work with two or three pupils

(v)   sufficient space overall in the school to allow for various forms of organisation of teaching groups

(vi)   imaginatively provided outdoor teaching and recreation spaces.

6.43   Additionally, when children with special needs are present, the ordinary class base should have:

(i)   space to allow a child with special needs to work at an appropriate pace without undue pressure from the movement of those around him, and to allow for an additional adult

(ii)   additional storage space to hold a slightly augmented range of teaching material and equipment

(iii) sufficient electric sockets for the use of special teaching aids.

6.44   The internal environment should meet the requirements set out in Design Note 17[1] for lighting and acoustic conditions, particularly in regard to the reduction of noise levels in teaching spaces and sound insulation between rooms. Basic requirements for access should also be met (see paragraphs 4.66–67).

6.45   The following examples show how existing primary schools, which have these supportive features and were designed to meet these criteria, might be adapted to accommodate children with special educational needs. (The fact that they have been selected as examples is not intended to imply that there are necessarily children with special educational needs in them at present.) The examples show how

some support areas might be provided in suitable spaces in the school. If this were to be done, and no new building were added, the capacity of the school as a whole would be reduced; the implications of this are discussed fully in Chapter 9.

6.46   Some examples of how practical and other teaching areas might be adapted to provide access for the physically disabled are given at the end of the chapter.

---

1.   *Guidelines for Environmental Design and Fuel Conservation in Educational Buildings.* Design Note 17, DES, 1981.

A remodelled infant school

6.47 Figure 14a illustrates a pre-1903 school building which has been remodelled[1] to provide greater variety in type of teaching space and more up-to-date area standards for each class group.

Provision for all children with special educational needs

6.48 The two fully self-contained class bases with adjoining quiet rooms would provide a settled environment for infant classes which include one or two pupils with special needs. The two paired class bases with adjacent practical areas and quiet room which are slightly more spacious overall, could well accommodate an extra teacher or adult helper(s) working with the groups. Two of the quiet rooms (one off the hall) have separate access and either could be used from time to time for withdrawal of pupils from any class group. There is easy access to a terrace for outdoor work/play from four of the class bases. A hand-shower and sink need to be available near one group of lavatories.

6.49 For individual or small group work, special needs teaching or speech therapy, a number of quiet rooms are available as well as the MI room. The quiet room next to Base 1 with an adjacent store would be particularly suitable. Aids, equipment and resources

could then be stored when not in use so that Base 1 could continue its normal use of the quiet room for class stories etc. The store is daylit and could be used for preparation of learning aids to meet individual children's needs.

Children with sensory handicaps

6.50 For visually handicapped and hearing impaired children the hall would present some problems initially. A large space with doors leading off it in various positions is not ideal for partially sighted and blind pupils, and the stairs to the library on the mezzanine floor could be a hazard, although the surfaces are well lit. It is a large reverberant space, as found in many existing primary schools, and thus handicapping to hearing impaired pupils. It might be necessary to consider additional acoustic treatment, or providing the children with extra support when they are using this area.

Access for the physically disabled

6.51 The majority of doors and doorways are accessible to wheelchair users, having a minimum clear opening width of 750mm. With the exception of the library on the mezzanine floor the school is on one level. Externally ramps provide access to the main entrance and terrace.

---

1. Described in Broadsheet 3, *Remodelling of Jackfield School*, DES, 1980.

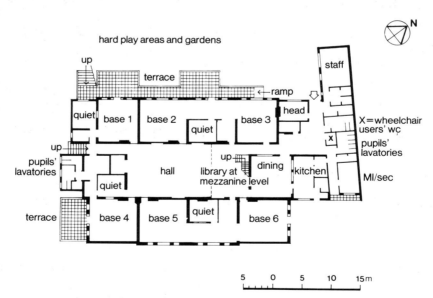

Figure 14a. A remodelled infant school

6.52 Pupils' lavatories are located at both ends of the school building. A WC suitable for wheelchair users is located close to the main entrance and the MI room. Figure 14b illustrates a modified layout to the lavatories adjoining Bases 1 and 4, which provides a changing bench and hand-shower facility suitable for physically disabled pupils.

6.53 Teaching Bases 5 and 6 have been furnished in Figure 14c to illustrate access into and around the spaces for a pupil using a wheelchair. Figure 14c also shows how some of the existing bench seating in the dining area might be replaced by loose chairs, which together with a suitable table height allows access for wheelchair users. A parking area for wheelchairs or walking aids might be provided for pupils able to use the ordinary dining furniture.

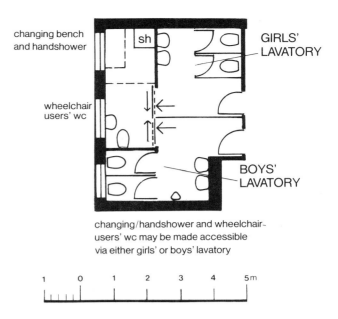

changing/handshower and wheelchair-users' wc may be made accessible via either girls' or boys' lavatory

Figure 14b. Modifications to pupils' lavatories in a remodelled infant school

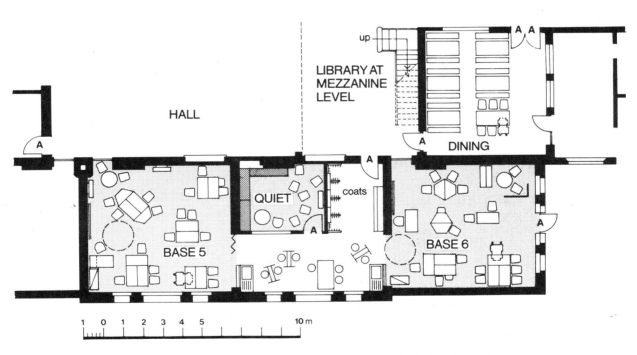

Figure 14c. Access within Bases 5 and 6 and dining area of remodelled infant school

Provision of a support space

6.54 When a support space in the form of a classroom is required, the two most suitable positions for it are Bases 1 and 4, which have integral practical facilities, immediate access to a quiet room and lavatories quite near. Base 1, although the smallest (39m^2), has the advantage that the outside paved area links to those of other groups. If a secluded outdoor area is considered an advantage, for example for very young pupils or for the particular needs of the majority of pupils using the support space, Base 4 might be selected. Also, if any pupil in this group uses a wheelchair or other mobility aid, Base 4 would be easier to enter and move about in. For hearing impaired children to use either of these bases more carpet would have to be provided to help sound absorption and the walls should be acoustically treated. An additional door would be fitted to form a sound lobby.

6.55　Figure 14d shows how Base 1 might be furnished for up to six hearing impaired pupils (for details of furniture, equipment, etc, see Figure 9). An alternative arrangement of the same room (Figure 14e) shows how it might provide a suitable support area for eight to ten pupils with moderate learning difficulties (for details see Figure 7a). Although the room is small for the full range of activities for this number of pupils it can be supplemented by the use of the adjoining quiet room.

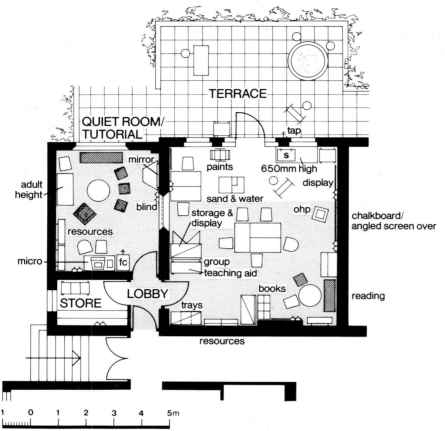

Figure 14d.　Base 1 of remodelled infant school furnished for hearing impaired pupils

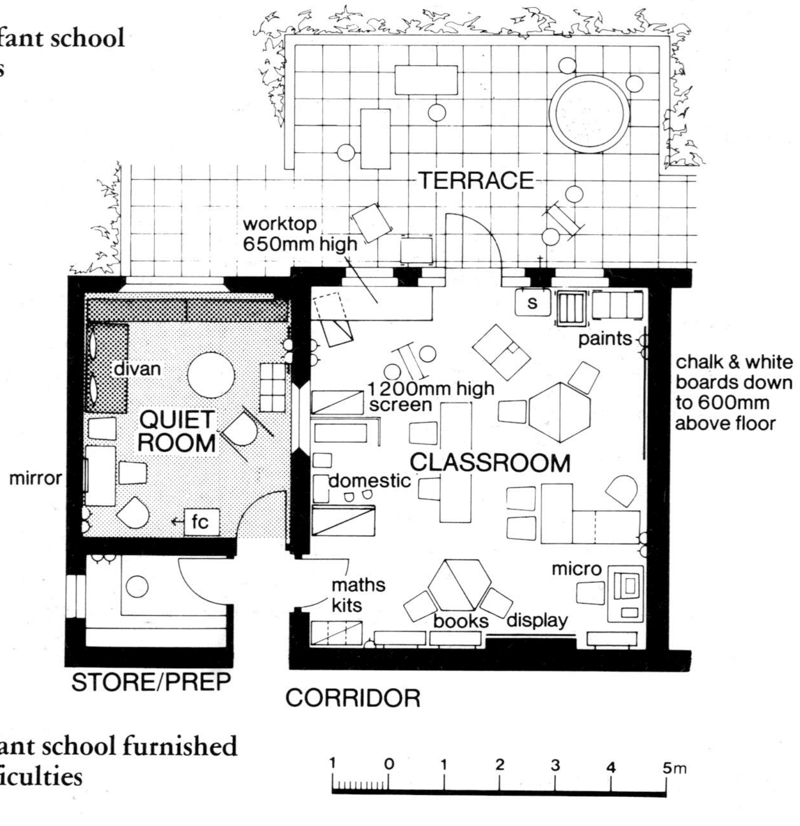

Figure 14e.　Base 1 of remodelled infant school furnished for pupils with moderate learning difficulties

A junior school

6.56 Figure 15a illustrates a junior school built in 1976 for up to 420 pupils.[1] A range of spaces is provided for general work in teaching clusters. These each include a general learning area with practical investigation nuclei, a small group room and a large group room. The four large group rooms, two of which are provided with a sink, may operate as self-contained classrooms or as language or mathematics rooms. The bases in the general learning area are clearly defined semi-open areas.

Provision for all children with special educational needs

6.57 The advantage of this range of spaces (described in paragraph 6.56) is the opportunity to choose a self-contained enclosed base for a class containing one or two pupils with special needs; or,

where it is likely that the teaching team will be augmented, three teachers or more could operate in the shared base areas with different size groups for part of the time.

6.58 In addition to quiet rooms distributed among teaching bases, the tutorial room is suitable for one-to-one work, while for individual work the library has study bays and electric sockets for the use of learning apparatus.

6.59 There are a number of other features in this school which would be particularly supportive for children with special needs, in particular the small cookery bay where a child may receive help from either a parent or a member of staff, the drama / music room, and the clay / craft room with outside work area.

6.60 The school has a good range of storage provision and an adult work bay for preparation of teaching resources, sited near the staff room.

---

1. Described in Building Bulletin 56, *Guillemont Junior School, Farnborough, Hampshire*, HMSO, 1976.

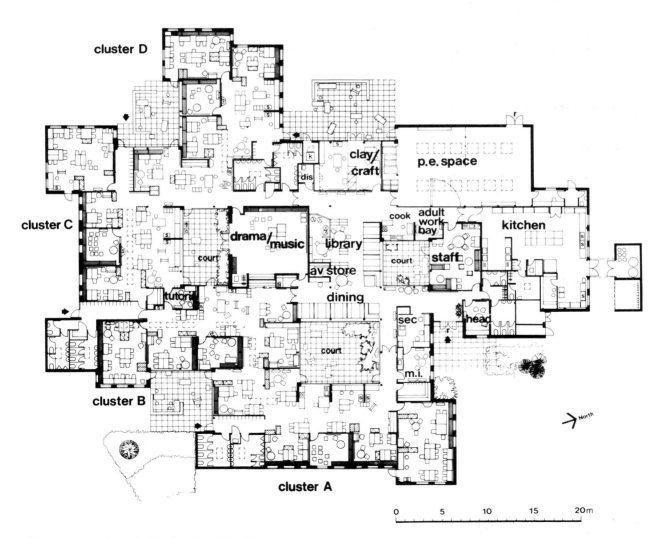

Figure 15a. An existing junior school

6.61   The design of the internal environment, including lighting and acoustics, follows DES guidance and produces quiet comfortable conditions. Many of the teaching spaces have good natural lighting with windows on two or more sides. Space for an additional adult may be required when pupils are working in the practical investigation areas or the clay/craft room. The MI or tutorial room could, with acoustic wall treatment if necessary, also be used for auditory training and speech and language work for hearing impaired pupils.

6.62   The building is semi-open plan and the layout makes it suitable for pupils with visual handicap. There is at least one straightforward route to each of the teaching clusters. There are several well lit sitting positions on the perimeter of each teaching area for more difficult and demanding tasks which require particularly good lighting. Additional task lighting could be provided as required.

Access for the physically disabled

6.63   Access into and around the school is suitable for wheelchair users, with adequate width to all doorways in teaching and circulation areas and external doors. The school is on one level with suitably ramped external access. A lavatory suitable for wheelchair users (adults or pupils) is located centrally in the school with access from the general circulation area. The three groups of pupils' lavatories are accessible to ambulant physically disabled pupils.

6.64   Figures 15b and 15c illustrate some alternative furniture layout studies to include a pupil using a wheelchair or other space-consuming mobility aid. Generally with the minimum spacings indicated it should be possible for such pupils to participate freely in the activity of an ordinary class, without impediment to either themselves or fellow pupils. Space may also be required for wheelchair parking. In these examples a 400mm 'chair zone' is indicated around tables as a guide to space planning. (See also Figure A6.)

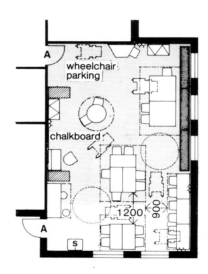

Figure 15b.   Junior class base: access study

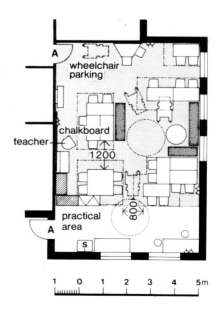

Figure 15c.   Junior class base: access study

6.65   It would be possible to site a two-teacher support centre for pupils with moderate learning difficulties in this school if required, as the school is large enough for these children to be registered in mainstream classes in small numbers. Two classroom/resource areas could be used, where these children would spend part of their time. The most suitable siting among the teaching areas would be the large self-contained classroom in Cluster A and the smaller one in Cluster D, each for a two-year age span. Practical facilities are available in general areas adjacent to the latter, and there is an adjoining quiet or story room, used at different times by each teaching group in the cluster. The spaces therefore offer various opportunities for working in other groups. Figure 15d shows how the classroom in Cluster A might be furnished for this purpose.

6.66   If only one class area was required as a support teaching space for extraction of eight to twelve pupils with special needs at a time, the most appropriate site would be the classroom in Cluster B; storage, one-to-one room and practical facilities are close by and it is equally accessible from both halves of the school.

6.67   Other facilities that would be available to support these pupils include the MI room, which could be furnished suitably for one-to-one work and for speech therapy, and the adult work bay and storage area available for preparation and storage of learning material. A small shower facility for these pupils would be most useful, although in common with many junior schools of the time this would need to be added.

6.68   Alternatively, if a support classroom for pupils with sensory handicaps were to be provided, the classroom in Cluster D would be suitable, as it is well lit on three sides. It is adjacent both to a practical area with a sink and to a quiet room which can be used for one-to-one and small group work, when not being used by children in adjacent bases. The enclosed room in Cluster A is equally suitable, being well lit and already provided with a sink; it is adjacent to a store and the MI room is close at hand. The classroom in Cluster B is well located between pairs of teaching clusters and is close to the tutorial room, but it is immediately adjacent to a corridor/coats area which could be noisy, and although there is rooflighting, windows are only provided at one end of the classroom.

6.69   Figure 15e shows how the classroom in Cluster D might be furnished as a support area for hearing impaired pupils, or other children who may require additional language and reading tuition; it would have to be modified with acoustic wall treatment to improve listening conditions. (For details of furniture and equipment see Figure 9.) Alternatively, the same classroom could be furnished as a support area for a small group of visually handicapped pupils (see Figure 10).

Figure 15d. Junior classroom furnished for 8 to 12 pupils with moderate learning difficulties

Figure 15e. Junior classroom furnished for up to 8 hearing impaired pupils

Access within practical and other common teaching spaces for the physically disabled

6.70 Figures 16a–d show ways in which a pupil in a wheelchair may use these areas. The spaces illustrated are in a recently designed 300 place middle school, where some of the practical areas also serve as class bases.

Science area/class base

6.71 The class base shown in Figure 16a has an adjacent science nucleus for use in conjunction with the class base or separately. Wheelchair passing widths as illustrated allow access to most areas and groups. There is a 700mm high table in both areas for a pupil seated in a wheelchair.

Figure 16. Access studies in a primary school

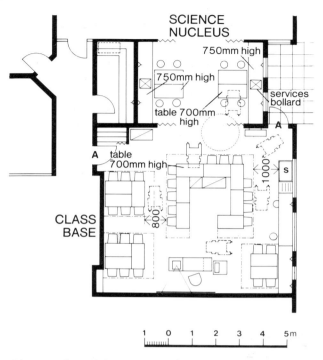

Figure 16a. Science area / class base

Audiovisual/music room

6.72 In Figure 16b the larger room has been designed for audiovisual and music activities. The seating layout shown is for an audiovisual presentation, and provided a clear gangway is maintained a pupil in a wheelchair will have access to a choice of seating positions. There is also adequate space within the room to park a wheelchair.

6.73 The layout in the smaller room is for individual work at carrels or for a small group. While, with this layout, there is no space to park a wheelchair, a pupil working from a wheelchair has access to either an adjustable height carrel or group table positions, if a 700mm floor to work surface height is provided.

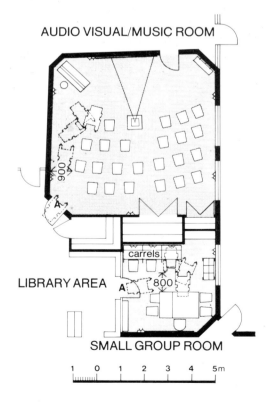

Figure 16b. Audiovisual / music room and small group room

Home studies area/class base

6.74 The class base shown in Figure 16c has an adjacent home studies nucleus for use in conjunction with the class base or separately. The passing widths illustrated allow access to a choice of working positions and groups. There is a 700mm high table in the class base for a pupil seated in a wheelchair.

6.75 The home studies nucleus for a group of up to eight pupils is equipped with two cookers and two sinks with worktops. A sink with user-controlled height adjustment (see Figure 29g) together with a trolley-mounted electric hob (approximately 700mm high) would enable a pupil in a wheelchair to be more easily included in a working group.

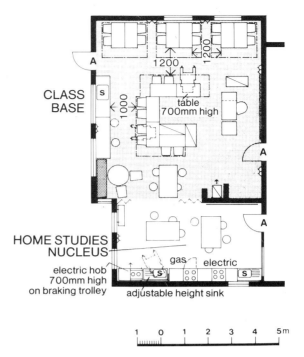

Figure 16c. Home studies area / class base

Clay/craft area

6.76 Designed as a clay and craft area for up to 15 pupils, the room shown in Figure 16d is equipped with wall benching, racks, storage and sinks for a variety of activities including wood and metalwork, clay/pottery, enamelling etc. Three craft tables at 750mm high are shown, although for particular pupils working from wheelchairs it may be preferable to include at least one table or workbench at a lower height of 700mm.

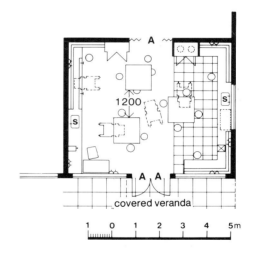

Figure 16d. Clay / craft area

7. Secondary School Accommodation

7.1 At secondary level, as at primary, there is a need for support spaces to be provided for children with special educational needs, and some examples of these are given below. However, there will also be a need for pupils to participate in the far more varied activities of the school, and to work with many more teachers than at primary level. The support spaces must therefore be seen as complementary to the rest of the school's accommodation. A guide to the type and range of accommodation that will be helpful in the school as a whole will be found in paragraphs 7.23–28. At the end of the chapter, some examples are given of how access may be provided for physically disabled pupils both to the whole school and within various teaching spaces.

Design studies: examples of support spaces

Small study and preparation areas

7.2 Secondary schools usually have staff workrooms and reprographic facilities. However, when these are not available, or where additional teaching material has to be prepared, suitable provision must be made. In Figure 17, a variety of small support areas are shown, providing a combination of preparation, storage and small study areas designed to supplement the existing school accommodation.

7.3 In the smallest of these examples, there is space for an individual pupil and tutor to work in a tutorial room; the largest provides a small suite of tutorial, study and preparation rooms. All examples include a small store, while provision may also incorporate study carrels, lockable storage for aids and equipment, facilities for maintenance of hearing aids, and secretarial support when required for typing, brailling etc. The tutorial room could be used for speech work if provided with suitable acoustic treatment.

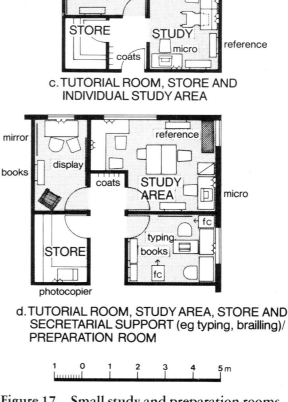

c. TUTORIAL ROOM, STORE AND
   INDIVIDUAL STUDY AREA

d. TUTORIAL ROOM, STUDY AREA, STORE AND
   SECRETARIAL SUPPORT (eg typing, brailling)/
   PREPARATION ROOM

a. TUTORIAL ROOM AND
   LOCKABLE STORE

b. TUTORIAL ROOM AND
   STORE/PREPARATION
   ROOM

Figure 17. Small study and preparation rooms
in a secondary school

Support classrooms

Pupils with moderate learning difficulties

7.4   Figure 18 shows two support classrooms, one for the lower and one for the upper school. (See also paragraph 4.23.)

7.5   In the lower school classroom in Figure 18a, there is sufficient space for eight to ten pupils and a range of activities are catered for. The room opens on to an outdoor terrace. A small quiet room adjoins for work with individuals or small groups. A lockable walk-in store for small aids/audiovisual trolley etc is immediately available.

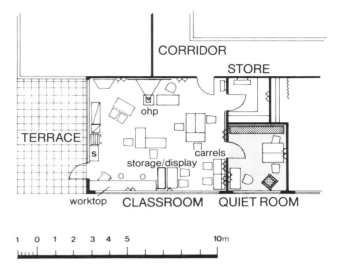

Figure 18a.   Support classroom in a secondary school for pupils with moderate learning difficulties (lower school)

7.6   For the upper school, Figure 18b shows a classroom primarily for 'non-practical' subjects, although a sink is needed, and an adjoining resource/study room for individual work and storage/display of specific reference material. The main classroom will accommodate a group of eight to ten pupils with special needs and when not being used by them can accommodate a group of up to 15 other pupils.

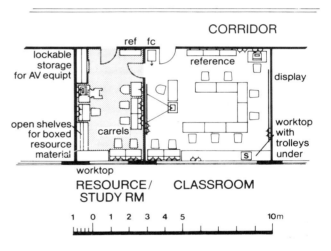

Figure 18b.   Support classroom in a secondary school for pupils with moderate learning difficulties (upper school)

7.7 Figures 19 and 20 show support classrooms for up to eight hearing impaired and visually handicapped pupils respectively (see also paragraph 4.35). Both are designed to be used to back up work in mainstream classes, with emphasis on individual or small group specialised teaching according to age, level of attainment and special needs. In each case there is therefore one general teaching area, a smaller tutorial/individual workroom, a study bay, and a store. The furniture shown will allow for different teaching needs. In the area designed for hearing impaired pupils, furniture is illustrated in a 'horseshoe' for a group doing basic language and communication work, but could also be laid out for small group and individual work. In both examples the classroom has a sink and worktop, and the internal environment conforms to the standards recommended in Design Note 25 (see paragraphs 4.38–43).

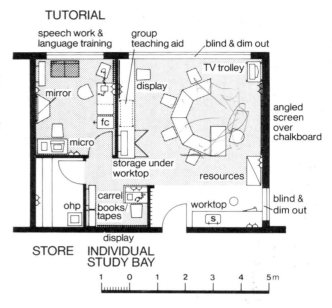

Figure 19. Support classroom for hearing impaired pupils in a secondary school

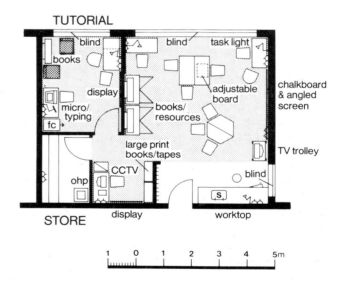

Figure 20. Support classroom for visually handicapped pupils in a secondary school

Pupils with emotional and behavioural disorders

7.8   In Figure 21 a classroom of 70m² has been converted for use by a group of eight–ten pupils. The space allows for a flexible layout so that individual work places can be formed with divider screens; a worktop and sink are provided. There is a study bay with carrels, an enclosed quiet room for withdrawal, and a lockable store for audiovisual aids and other vulnerable items. (See also paragraphs 4.57–58.)

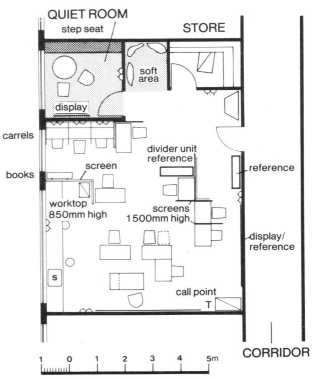

Figure 21.   Support classroom for pupils with emotional and behavioural disorders in a secondary school

Older pupils or leavers

7.9   When pupils with special educational needs are in mainstream classes for the earlier years of secondary school, a classroom may still be needed where older pupils or leavers, including those with special educational needs of any kind, may spend part of their time (see paragraph 4.21). The classroom shown in Figure 22 is designed to supplement existing formal class bases and practical rooms. The aim is to provide an atmosphere that reflects the greater maturity and growth to independence of these pupils, providing appropriate social and learning activities.

7.10   The room shown here could be closely linked to other resource areas in the school including the library, and also usefully to the school home economics or craft areas. It provides spaces for individual study, counselling, discussion, and display of specific reference material (on careers etc), and there is a social area with a small cooking bay.

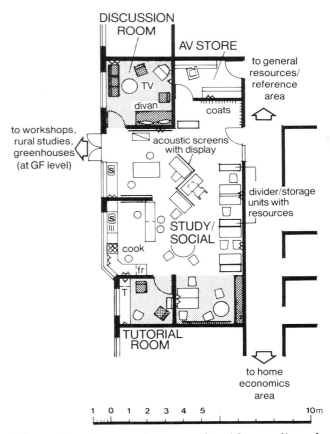

Figure 22.   Support classroom for older pupils and leavers in a secondary school

43

Support centres

Support centres for pupils with moderate learning difficulties

7.11   Figures 23 and 24 both show centres for a large number of pupils with moderate learning difficulties (see also paragraph 4.25). Appropriately designed centres are most easily (but not exclusively) achieved in new building, and are thus ideally provided in an extension or new building phase; but at the same time the aim should be to ensure that a centre thus provided is as integral to other facilities as possible rather than isolated from the rest of the school.

7.12   In both cases, the centre would be used for only part of the time by pupils with moderate learning difficulties registered in mainstream classes. The centre may therefore help pupils with milder learning difficulties at other times. Equally the social areas can also be seen as adding to the total social provision of the school, and might be used in breaks by pupils using the centre, and their friends.

7.13   The two examples differ in the types of teaching accommodation provided. However, depending on the existing facilities of the school, the kind of provision in the smaller example might be appropriate in a larger centre, and vice versa. In both

there is provision for individual study in serviced carrels.

7.14   It is possible that one or two pupils using wheelchairs will be taught for some of their time in such a centre. In this case the cookery bay could well have an adjustable height sink and / or worktop, as suggested in Figure 29g. In the craft area, space around the benches could be needed as detailed in Figure 29e.

7.15   Provision of facilities outdoors, to extend the range of work being done in the centre, could include a covered craft or projects area, growing areas, and access to, for example, rural studies areas where these are part of the general school provision.

7.16   Figure 23 shows a four- or five-teacher support centre with approximately 45–60 work spaces. There is one self-contained classroom (44m^2) with simple practical facilities, perhaps for younger pupils, one of 37m^2, and a range of spaces where, for instance, a home skills project or practical investigation work can take place. Acoustically separate rooms for discussion and tutorials open off the main teaching area.

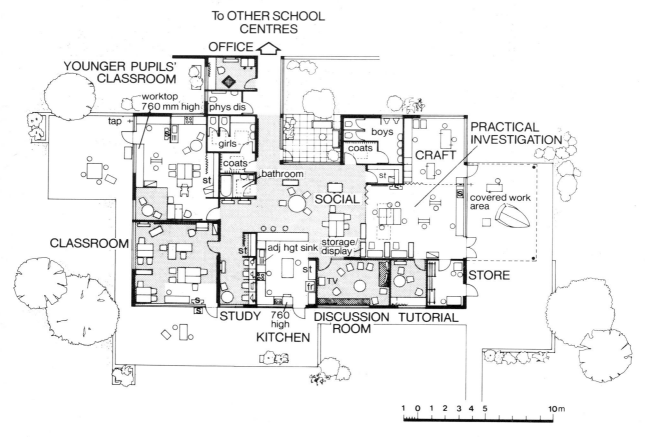

Figure 23.   Support centre for pupils with moderate learning difficulties in a secondary school

7.17   Figure 24 shows a centre potentially for six teachers which can function with five teachers or more. Other adults may also be present. Work spaces are provided for 60–70 pupils. There are two classrooms of approximately 42m², a larger one of 50m² with a sink and experimental bay, and an enclosed room for light and/or heavier craft. There is a small base for cookery (supplementing existing provision in the school) and the central area can be rearranged for home studies, preparation for a camping weekend, etc.

7.18   The centre has lavatory provision for the numbers that will be working in it, although in some existing schools this degree of additional provision will not be necessary. A small room is available for occasional short rest, for example by a pupil with epilepsy, and a WC and shower are available to physically disabled pupils working in the centre. It is assumed that any more extensive provision for the medical/care needs of physically disabled pupils who may be using the centre will be available elsewhere in the school, perhaps in or near the central MI area.

7.19   Important ancillary areas include adequate lockable storage for teaching material and equipment, and a staff workroom large enough for preparation of material.

7.20   In addition to the 60–70 pupils for whom the centre is designed, it may also help some 30–40 pupils who have milder learning difficulties.

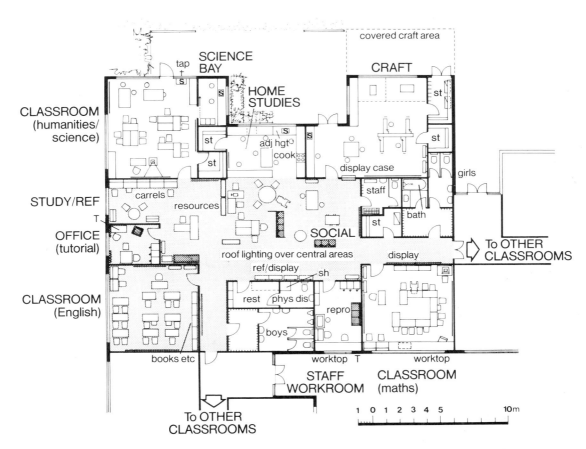

Figure 24.   Support centre for pupils with moderate learning difficulties in a secondary school

7.21 Figure 25 shows a support centre for up to 16 pupils with hearing impairment (see also paragraph 4.35). It consists of one classroom with worktop and sink, a smaller teaching space which could also be used for discussion, individual study and small groups, a tutorial room suitable for speech training, and a store/preparation space. The centre is assumed to be complementary to areas for subject teaching in the main school.

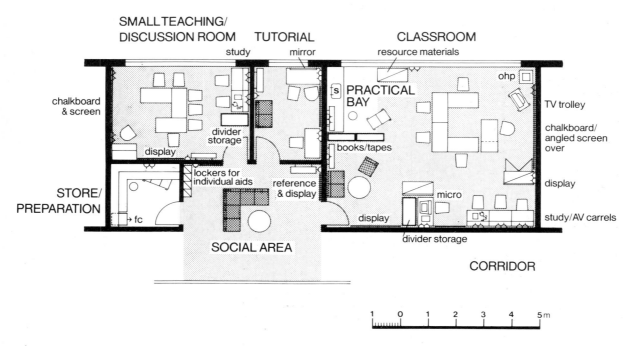

Figure 25. **Support centre for hearing impaired pupils in a secondary school**

7.22   The centre shown in Figure 26 would provide
accommodation for about 16 pupils who would at
some stage be spending most of their time in the
centre, and therefore caters for a wider range of
activities than a support classroom (see paragraph
4.59). The accommodation includes a general
classroom with sink and worktop; a smaller group
room; a quiet discussion/noisy social room with soft
finishes; a small enclosed craft support area; lockable
storage; a small kitchen/home studies support bay
linked to a social/study area; and a room for
individual teaching and counselling.

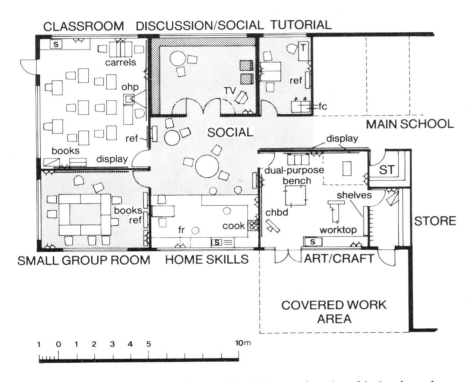

**Figure 26.   Support centre for pupils with emotional and behavioural
disorders in a secondary school**

Whole school accommodation

7.23   Where support spaces are required, the pupils using them will also spend a proportion of their time in mainstream classes. Even if support spaces are not required, there will be pupils with special educational needs in the school for whom appropriate educational provision must be made, and the accommodation in the school as a whole should therefore take account of these needs. (The area implications of the recommendations made below are discussed in Chapter 9.)

7.24   Provision for meeting pupils' special educational needs will require a response from all subject departments, involving changes in method, organisation, resources and accommodation. A range of accommodation that can meet these needs is required. The timetabling of teaching groups, and also individuals, is assisted if all general teaching subject areas have a variety of sizes of space, and if some classrooms have a worktop and sink for aspects of practical work. A group room such as that shown in Figure 27 has space for practical work and individual study.

7.25   In home economics and craft areas, it is an advantage if some less committed space is available, so that provision can be made for more differentiated activities, matching the range of ability in given teaching groups. In home economics for example, a variety of types of space is particularly helpful. In CDT (craft, design and technology) accommodation an uncommitted space allows some pupils to work on large projects at an appropriate pace. Similarly, in science areas, spaces suitable for general science are necessary, as is easy access to a space for audiovisual presentation. Art and music areas, if well designed for all pupils, will also provide for the needs of pupils with special educational needs, for whom this area of experience is valuable.

7.26   The school may have a central learning resource centre, ie an extended library with audiovisual and other forms of resource material, with suitable equipment and study areas with serviced carrels for individuals and small groups to use the resources. Whether central or departmentally based, some pupils with learning difficulties can receive additional support in such an area.

7.27   Many secondary schools do not yet provide such a helpful mix of accommodation. Classrooms too often provide for a restricted range of teaching method and learning activity, and specialist spaces are often closely orientated to particular skills. In such schools, the opportunity may arise, through local population growth or reorganisation, to extend or modify the range of accommodation available. In addition to providing a greater variety of spaces for

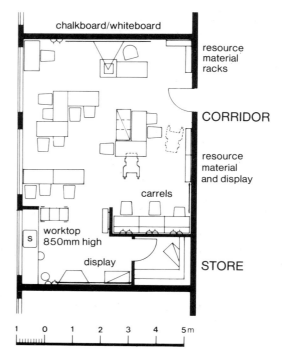

Figure 27.   General support room in a secondary school

activities in the general teaching areas as described above, the provision for practical subjects may need to be augmented, and this might be done either within departments or in the form of a study centre for older pupils. Such a centre, as shown in Figure 28, could be used for optional work, some of which could be organised thematically. Accommodating several groups, it would reduce the pressure on practical spaces, and would also provide a pastoral/social/ study area for those pupils who are approaching school leaving age.

7.28 A secondary school provided with such a range of accommodation, designed to support a variety of teaching methods and learning experiences, will be better placed to make the whole curriculum more accessible to pupils with special educational needs.

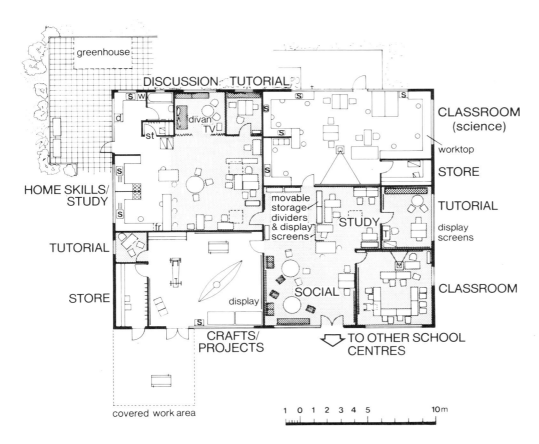

Figure 28. Study centre for older pupils in a secondary school

Access for the physically disabled

7.29   Paragraphs 4.64–71 discussed the need for access to meet pupils' full curriculum requirements, and the modifications which may be needed within teaching spaces. Figures 29a–g show how specialist subject areas might be adapted to suit their needs, while Figure 30 is an example of a school where access was required to the whole building, and shows the adaptations that have been carried out to make this possible.

Access to specialist subject areas

An existing general science laboratory

7.30   In Figure 29a, services and sinks are centrally located in bollards, and a lower science table (760mm high) is provided for a pupil seated in a wheelchair. A side worktop also at 760mm provides an alternative work station for such a pupil. Lower stools enable other pupils in the laboratory to use these work surfaces. The layout enables pupils in wheelchairs to view demonstration/experimental work and to join groups working around the bollards.

Figure 29.   Access studies in a secondary school

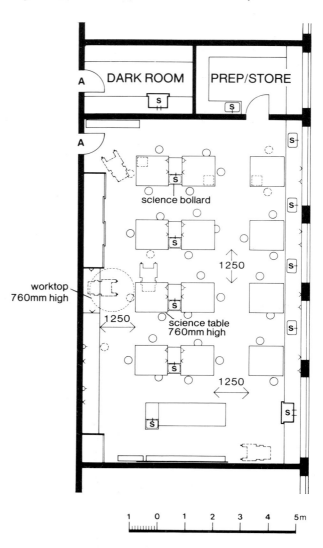

Figure 29a.   An existing general science laboratory

An existing chemistry laboratory and demonstration room

7.31 In Figure 29b, high fixed benching (820mm high), narrow aisles (760mm wide) and a raised demonstration bench, exacerbate the problems facing a pupil in a wheelchair and the modifications illustrated in Figures 29c and 29d benefit all users. Removal of the front fixed bench and the raised demonstration bench, and the substitution of either a science bollard (incorporating sink, gas and electrical services), or a science trolley similarly equipped, enable tables of varying heights to be used according to pupils' individual needs. In addition access around this area of the laboratory will have been improved.

7.32 The loose tables and chairs in the existing demonstration room adjoining the laboratory permit rearrangement to suit a pupil requiring additional space for a wheelchair. A less formal layout of tables is also possible.

CHEMISTRY LABORATORY   DEMONSTRATION ROOM

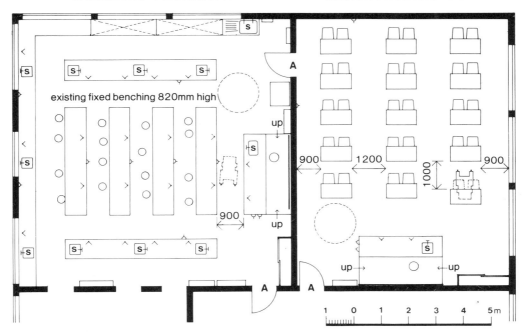

Figure 29b. An existing chemistry laboratory and demonstration room

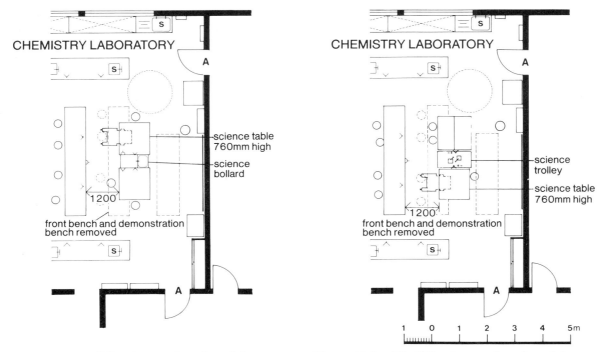

Figure 29c. Modification to chemistry laboratory   **Figure 29d.** Modification to chemistry laboratory

7.33 Part of the workshop shown in Figure 29e has been modified to create more space and a greater choice of working position for classes which include pupils with special needs, some of whom may have physical disabilities or difficulties with co-ordination. Three traditional workbenches (six work spaces) have been omitted and a four place adjustable group bench substituted. The normal bench height may be around 850mm, but for many craft activities a bench working height of around 700mm may be preferred by a pupil working from a wheelchair. Tool storage is located so as to leave clear space to allow close working. A pupil in a wheelchair has access to one workshop sink, lowered to a height of approximately 750mm with a clear space underneath.

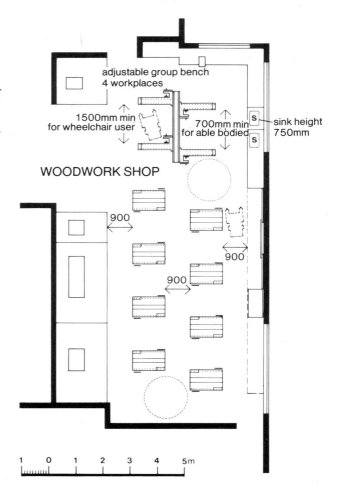

Figure 29e. An existing woodwork shop

7.34 Fittings at one end of the room as shown in Figure 29f have been modified in Figure 29g so that both able-bodied pupils and wheelchair users may use the same provision. A standard single-drainer sinktop, fitted with flexible waste and services, is supported on a wall-mounted sliding frame allowing a clear floor area below for the wheelchair. Immediate adjustment to the sink height – variable between 720mm and 900mm – is obtained by a simple lever controlled by the user. An adjacent worktop surface is similarly mounted. The work area is therefore suitable for any pupil working either individually or as part of a group. Other features included, with physically disabled pupils particularly in mind, are the low level electric hob 760mm high; a pull-out flap with hole for a mixing bowl; under-worktop storage trolley, and electric oven with side hung door. A standard domestic gas cooker with side hung oven door is sited nearby.

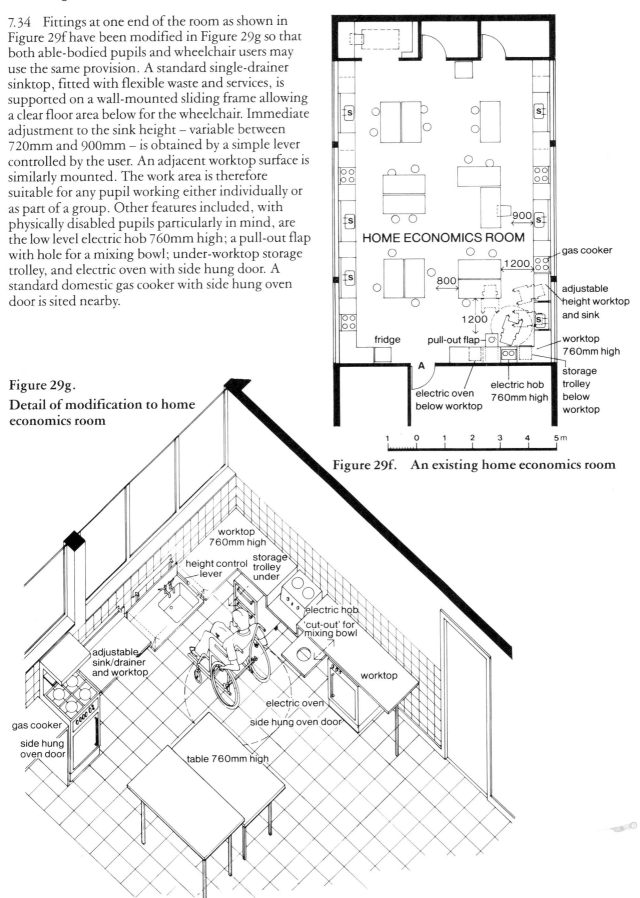

Figure 29g.

Detail of modification to home economics room

Figure 29f.   An existing home economics room

Access to the whole school

7.35 Figure 30 shows how an existing secondary school has been adapted to provide full access for physically disabled pupils.

7.36 There are approximately 1,100 pupils aged 11–18 in this school. In recent years the school has had eight to ten physically disabled pupils on roll at any one time. A maximum of six pupils dependent upon a wheelchair for mobility was envisaged, with a preferred maximum of four. However, these numbers have not in fact been reached in the school to date (1983).

7.37 Although the school site is relatively flat, extensive ramping was necessary to enable unaided wheelchair access to the main circulation routes. A mezzanine short-rise lift overcomes the change of level in the main entrance hall, and an eight-person passenger lift serving the ground, mezzanine and first floor levels is centrally located in the school. Both lifts are intended for unaided use by disabled pupils. Worn flooring in the corridor has been replaced with non-slip material to assist ambulant disabled pupils. In addition to a WC suitable for wheelchair users

Figure 30. An existing secondary school adapted to provide full access for physically disabled pupils

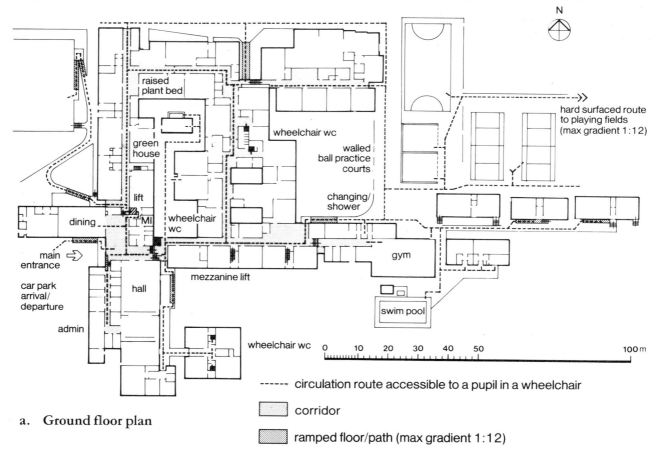

a. Ground floor plan

------ circulation route accessible to a pupil in a wheelchair

▨ corridor

▨ ramped floor/path (max gradient 1:12)

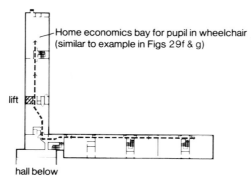

b. First floor plan

located near the main entrance and MI area, four similar WCs are distributed around the school at ground floor level.

7.38 In the majority of cases physically disabled pupils have been able to use standard school furniture without modifications. In some instances adaptations have been made, for example to work benches and in the provision of standing supports, enabling individual disabled pupils to use normal classroom and workshop facilities.

7.39 In this school, the agreed management arrangements for escape from the first floor include timetabling to ensure that only one pupil dependent on a wheelchair for mobility is upstairs at any one time. When the fire alarm rings, two 'designated' staff assist the pupil down the appropriate staircase and out of the building. Ambulant physically disabled pupils are guided out of the building by the teacher they are with.

8.   Care and Treatment Facilities

8.1   The normal provision in primary and secondary schools for medical examination and treatment (MI room) and for occasional rest, will meet the health care needs of all pupils, including a small number of individual children with special needs, provided that the size, layout and equipment are appropriate. Examples of such provision are shown in Figure 31 (see paragraphs 8.8–10).

8.2   This accommodation is usually located close to administrative rooms, and together with an attractive entrance and waiting and parents' area this offers a choice of rooms for discussion with a range of visiting specialists.

8.3   Sometimes visiting specialists will need to work with one or more pupils at a time using specialist material or equipment in a suitable small room; at other times they may be working with a pupil or with a class teacher in other parts of the school. Provision should be made for both situations. However, the requirements for these activities will vary and demands on specific space or specialist equipment will not be constant. It would be helpful therefore if any such specific space were suitable for small group activities of a kind that would still allow it to be used for its main purpose when required.

Provision for physiotherapy

8.4   For some children, especially the youngest, physiotherapy may be included in the class activity – eg in a nursery class. For the majority of primary or secondary pupils, physiotherapy if required will occur as an integrated part of their regular physical education programme. Additionally, at primary level, two or three pupils may be treated together by the visiting physiotherapist in any suitable 'uncommitted' area of the school eg music/drama room or small group room. However, for some pupils there is a need for some therapy necessitating privacy, for which a suitable withdrawal area will be required; the MI room, for example, should be capable of being used for individual therapy. Where the demand for physiotherapy is such as to warrant both privacy and the use of large apparatus not available in the physical education areas of the school, an additional area suitable for physiotherapy and the storage of equipment must be provided (see Figure 32).

Provision for speech therapy

8.5   Where the number of pupils requiring speech therapy is small, a tutorial room and/or the medical room could be used, provided that the space is suitably furnished, has suitable lighting and acoustic conditions, and has reasonable sound privacy from other spaces. Storage for the speech therapist's equipment and files is required, whether the therapist works with pupils on a withdrawal basis or in teaching situations around the school.

8.6   When there are larger numbers of pupils requiring speech therapy and for whom a special support teaching area is being provided, this area will include a small room designed for a number of functions but suitably arranged and equipped for speech therapy (see Figures 7 and 8).

8.7   For pupils with hearing impairment or speech and language disorders, both of whom need more critical room conditions, rooms specifically designed for speech work are included in their support areas (see Figures 9, 12, 19 and 25).

Examples

8.8 Figure 31a shows an MI room in a primary school suitable for use by the visiting doctor/school nurse. It has space for a folding couch, filing cabinet, weighing machine, vision testing card and mirror, desk and several chairs. A washhand basin and lockable first-aid cabinet are required. A minimum clear floor space is indicated for a physiotherapy mat. A store for physiotherapy aids and a WC suitable for use by a person in a wheelchair are sited nearby.

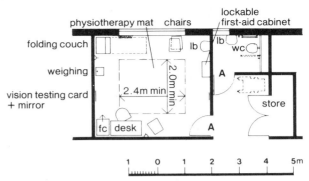

Figure 31a. An MI room in a primary school

8.9 Figure 31b illustrates the same room equipped for the purposes described above, but arranged also for speech therapy. Equipment for the latter could be housed in an adjoining store.

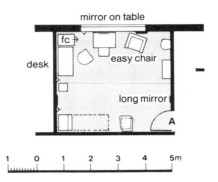

Figure 31b. Primary school MI room arranged for speech therapy

8.10 Figure 31c shows a design to meet the medical accommodation requirements of a secondary school. It includes a room for the visiting doctor, with space for a folding couch, vision testing card and mirror, a desk and several chairs. A washhand basin and lockable first-aid cabinet are required. The adjoining room for the school nurse includes a washhand basin, filing cabinet, weighing machine, space for a pupil requiring temporary rest, a desk and chairs. Where individual physiotherapy is needed one of the rooms should be large enough to provide a clear floor space similar to that shown in Figure 31a. A separate pupils' rest room and a WC which can be used by a pupil in a wheelchair are nearby. A hand-shower or bathing facility together with a bench for changing may also be required for some pupils with special needs.

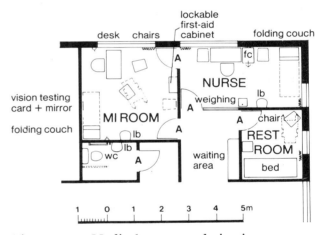

Figure 31c. Medical accommodation in a secondary school

8.11 Figure 32 shows a room suitable for physiotherapy: it has a free floor area of at least 15m² and a storage area with fitted shelving and wall hooks. A writing table and chairs are provided. There would need to be a WC nearby suitable for use by a pupil in a wheelchair.

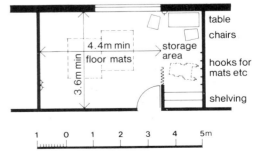

Figure 32. Physiotherapy room: primary and secondary schools

9.   Special Needs and the Capacity of Ordinary Schools

9.1   The minimum teaching area (MTA) required in schools is specified in the Education (School Premises) Regulations 1981.[1] Regulation 8 (2) requires that teaching accommodation for children in special schools shall be such as takes account of their special educational needs. The Regulations contain no reference to children with special educational needs who are admitted to ordinary schools, but as the Regulations relate to minimum requirements it is open to authorities to make additional provision for them.

9.2   At present schools, teachers, parents, and educational administrators are in the process of adapting to the new situation, and it is not an appropriate time to set new definitive standards. However, considerable thought has been given in the course of this study to the advice that should be given about teaching area in order to facilitate the changes in provision that are being made. During the investigation many visits were made to ordinary schools in which children with special educational needs were participating in many aspects of the school's work, and the prerequisite conditions were seen to be:

   (i)   that space was available both to serve as a base for the special resources provided, ie teachers with special training, aides, equipment and teaching materials; and for some or all of those children with special needs to meet from time to time;

   (ii) that space was available in the ordinary school for the special needs children to be in classes with other children in an appropriate size of teaching group.

9.3   These two conditions for successful provision are different in nature when considering a building brief. The first has been examined in detail in this Building Bulletin and the examples illustrated here cover the range of educational provision. **As a working generalisation it can be said that a gross area of about 75m² will include the teaching area, storage, circulation and administrative accommodation necessary to provide support for one full-time special teacher. Where provision is needed for peripatetic teacher support for a small number of children a smaller area of about 25m² is appropriate.** (These recommendations are based on area per teacher rather than per pupil, because the number of children

needing such provision varies according to age, and degree and nature of the disability.)

9.4   There is an exception to the generalisation where provision is made for more than one group of children with emotional and behavioural disorders, where the support centre provides for a wide range of activities (see Figure 26).

9.5   Physically disabled children, whether or not they attract provision for a special teacher, will nevertheless require additional area for **paramedical and personal care facilities** (see Figures 31a, 31c, 32, and A1–A3). For initial planning, before the development of detail, a gross area of about 75m² should be allowed for this purpose dependent upon the number of such pupils. However, if there are considerably more physically disabled pupils in a particular school than has been generally envisaged in this Building Bulletin, there could be a significant effect on circulation areas and on sizes of groups in teaching spaces. In such cases more gross area would be needed in the whole school.

9.6   The second precondition affects the brief of the ordinary school and requires assumptions to be made about teaching groups that include children with special needs. There seems to be a consensus that these groups need to be smaller than other groups to take account not only of the fact that most children with special needs require more immediate space – many of them, for instance, work on a whole table rather than a half – but also of the need for greater teacher attention to the special need, which should not reduce the consideration given to other pupils. Smaller group sizes produce a larger number of teaching groups overall and thus a need for a larger number of spaces if the operation of the ordinary school is not to be adversely affected. In the field, primary schools were seen in which access to shared areas such as the hall by children with special needs was restricted, and secondary schools were seen in which they had little access to specialist areas such as craft, and where it was difficult for time in science laboratories to be allocated to them. **To satisfy this demand for space within the rest of the school a standard of provision is suggested whereby each special needs child admitted to the school requires, in addition to the support area for the special teacher, a teaching area twice that of an ordinary child. Alternatively, in addition to the support area for the special teacher, the capacity of the school is reduced by the number of children with special needs on roll at any time.** This should enable an additional

---

1.   SI No 909, HMSO, 1981.

uncommitted space to be provided in many primary schools, and enable secondary schools to organise so that all groups have access to the full range of accommodation.

9.7 To exemplify this guidance four cases are described:

(a) a new 420 place JMI which includes 20 children with special educational needs on roll;

(b) a primary school where there is a small number of individual pupils with special needs served by one peripatetic teacher;

(c) an existing two-form entry JMI remodelled to form a one-form entry JMI with provision for up to 12 children with special educational needs, and with other accommodation;

(d) a secondary school for 900 11–16 year old pupils, showing the effect on teaching area, capacity, and the number of class meetings possible if 20 pupils with special educational needs are admitted.

Example (a)

9.8 The ordinary 420 place JMI would have an MTA of:

$$
\begin{array}{lll}
300 \times 2.24m^2 & = & 672.0 \\
120 \times 2.43m^2 & = & \underline{291.6} \\
& = & \underline{963.6m^2}
\end{array}
$$

This MTA would be expected to provide the minimum of 14 class bases for 30 children, including general learning area, practical areas, shared quiet rooms, plus a hall and some other more specialist space.

9.9 With 20 children with special educational need included in the roll the teaching area would be calculated thus:

$$
\begin{array}{lll}
300 \times 2.24m^2 & = & 672.0 \\
120 \times 2.43m^2 & = & \underline{291.6} \\
& = & \underline{963.6}
\end{array}
$$

Additional teaching area for 20 children with special needs:

$$
\begin{array}{lll}
20 \times 2.29m^{2*} & = & \underline{45.8} \\
& = & \underline{1,009.4m^2}
\end{array}
$$

*ie 963.6 ÷ 420

9.10 This additional 45.8m² of teaching area would provide for an additional uncommitted floor space, eg a separate audiovisual/music/drama room that

would enable more teaching groups to be formed within the school without leading to excessive demands upon the communal spaces. In addition to this the support area for two special teachers of 150m² gross, with its own increment of teaching area, will be needed.

Example (b)

9.11 For this example it is assumed that the primary school has spare space which it is intended should be used to support a small number of pupils with special needs. Figures 4 and 5 show the building provision that is required: a small one-to-one teaching space for the peripatetic teacher, and a preparation and store room for special equipment and material. Few primary schools have suitable small spaces that are not either already committed for storage of resources, or needed under the revised regulations for staff and changing. It will therefore be necessary to form new spaces, probably by subdivision of an existing classroom, and this will provide, in addition to the 25m² for the support area for the peripatetic teacher, a supplementary space for the whole school, eg a library area.

9.12 The loss of original capacity will be directly related both to the loss of teaching area and to the number of children with special needs admitted. For instance, if 25m² of teaching area is lost, the capacity will be reduced by $25m^2 \div 1.8m^2 = 14$ pupils. This is in addition to a reduction in the capacity by the number of special needs pupils on roll; as in the previous example, this makes it possible to reduce the working size of groups.

Example (c)

9.13 An existing two-form entry JMI having a notional capacity of 405 pupils is illustrated in Figure 33a. This capacity was assessed by a method based upon MTA but adapted to provide teaching spaces for 30 pupils.[1]

9.14 This school is affected by falling rolls but is still required as a JMI and is to accept 12 children with special educational needs. Remodelling is intended to use the whole of the building and to provide a teaching environment comparable to a new school.

9.15 The fundamental decision is that the existing classrooms, mostly 44.6m² and too small for a group of 30 pursuing a full range of classroom activities, should be remodelled to form two spaces out of three. In addition a nursery group and a family centre are to

---

1. See the Department of Education and Science letter S 24/123/072 dated 5 February 1982. Teaching spaces have a maximum size of 54m², ie 30 × 1.8m².

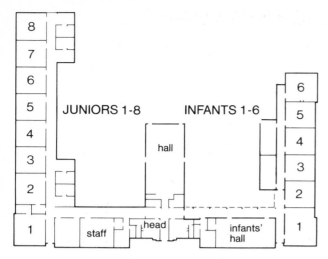

Figure 33a. A two-form entry JMI school

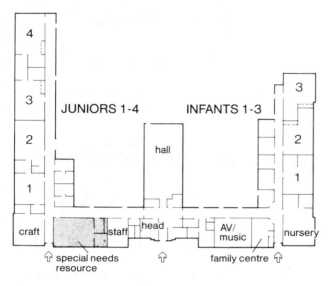

Figure 33b. The JMI school remodelled to include special needs support area

be provided and other deficiencies in balance area made good. The outline planning brief is illustrated in Figure 33b. As remodelled the notional capacity of the JMI, before adjusting for the children with special educational needs, is 255, largely because what may be considered a spare space exists – either the music/audiovisual space, or the clay/craft area. However, the effect of the 12 children with special educational needs is to reduce that figure to 243. If the school is staffed at a ratio of 25–26:1 upon the notional capacity the number of teachers will be 10 + 1 special teacher, which will enable those teaching groups which include pupils with special educational needs to be smaller.

Example (d)

9.16 In a new secondary school for 900 11–16 pupils, the minimum teaching area would normally be 3,654m^2. However, if the 900 was to include 20 children with special need, 81.2m^2 would be added to this, ie 20 × 3,654 ÷ 900, which could provide one or two additional teaching spaces. This is in addition to the spaces included in the 150m^2 provided to support the two special teachers.

9.17 If the ordinary school for 900 had 47 teaching spaces that allowed 1,600 meetings to take place in a 40 period week, then the average group size would be 900 × 40 ÷ 1,600 = 22.5 pupils. Should the additional space or spaces provided allow even only 36 more meetings to be held, then the average teaching group size could be reduced to 22.0 pupils. This would permit a reduction in the size of those groups in which children with special educational need were being taught. If these reductions were concentrated, they would permit considerable reduction in the size of, say, practical groups, in which these children were working.

9.18 If 20 children with special educational need were to be admitted to an existing school for 900 11–16 pupils without building an extension, the capacity of the school would need to be adjusted. Such a school would have 1,110 workplaces if its present capacity had been calculated on a workplace method. The support area for the two special teachers of 150m^2 would deprive the school of workplaces; it might displace 60, ie 150m^2 ÷ 2.47m^2 per workplace.[1] In addition two workplaces would be required for each child with special need, ie 20 × 1,110 ÷ 900 = 25. The school would thus lose a total of 85 workplaces, and its capacity[2] would be 1,025 × 75% = 767 + 7.7% = 825. **A working generalisation where special needs provision is made in an existing secondary school with no additional built area, is that the original pupil capacity will be reduced by four times the number of children with special need.**

9.19 Adding the support area by an extension to an existing school would reduce the original capacity directly by 20. This reduction in numbers will enable a comparable reduction in average group size, ie 22.5 × 880 ÷ 900 = 22.

---

1.   Average area per workplace excluding PE.

2.   See *Method for Assessing Capacity of Existing Schools,* DES, January 1982.

Appendix: Facilities for the Physically Disabled

Lavatory provision

A.1 Figure A1 is an example of lavatory and changing facilities designed to meet the normal day-to-day needs in a nursery school or class. In addition support rails and a washhand basin in the larger cubicle associated with the shower and changing bench, will aid the training for independence of a pupil with physical disabilities.

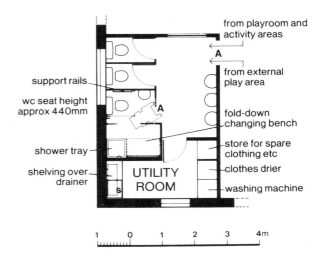

Figure A1. Lavatory and changing facility for physically disabled pupils of nursery age

A.2 Figure A2 is an example of a lavatory for boys in a secondary school which includes four WC cubicles, one of which is also suitable for a pupil in a wheelchair. One of the three bowl urinals has associated wall mounted vertical and horizontal rails for a pupil requiring temporary support.

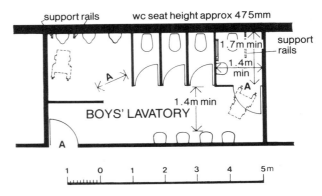

Figure A2. Lavatory provision for physically disabled pupils in secondary schools

A.3 Figure A3 shows a changing area in a secondary school physical education department with provision for a physically disabled pupil including 'parking area' for a wheelchair.

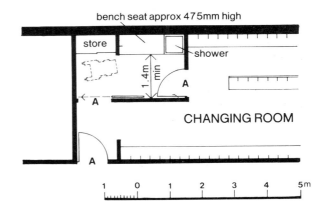

Figure A3. Changing area in a secondary school suitable for physically disabled pupils

Mobility aids and accessories room

A.4   Figure A4 illustrates two designs for the storage of mobility aids such as wheelchairs, walking frames, sticks and calipers, and for accessories such as foam wedges, cushions, detachable armrests, lap trays etc. Shelving with 'open access' and a parking area for a minimum of three wheelchairs are included. Where suitable facilities are not available elsewhere in the school a small bench may be provided as shown for minor adaptations and repairs. This room should be close to the pupils' main arrival and departure point and be easily accessible to pupils to store or retrieve wheelchairs etc. (Battery charging of powered wheelchairs should only take place in a space exclusively designed for it – see Figure A5.)

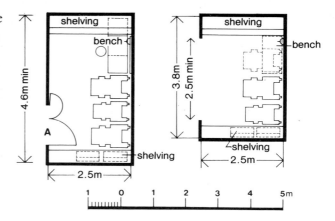

Figure A4.   Mobility aids and accessories rooms

Battery charging facilities

A.5   Figure A5 illustrates a room with provision for charging the batteries of up to three powered wheelchairs at any one time. Electric sockets are located above a shelf for battery chargers; the floor has acid resisting tiling and the room is permanently ventilated. A self-closing fire door separates the room from the school's circulation route. The recommendations of the Fire Prevention Officer should be sought when determining provision in and position of this room.

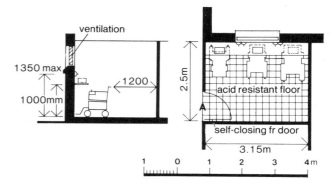

Figure A5.   Room for battery charging of wheelchairs

Furniture spacings and heights

A.6 The furniture spacings and heights etc illustrated in Figures A6 and A7 are intended only as a guide and reminder for designers and users. The minimum clear space for pupils dependent on wheelchairs or walking aids is indicated in Figure A6. In examples a–c and e–g of Figure A7, the table heights are those commonly found in junior or secondary classrooms. The preferred worktop heights (examples d and h) are lower than those required for pupils standing at worktops. As explained in Chapter 4, requirements will vary according to the pupil's disability and the specification of the wheelchair if needed – for instance, armrests, extended legrests, and the type and location of chair controls on powered wheelchairs, may affect the position of a chair in relation to table height. The design of existing furniture (eg the position of table legs) must also be considered. Space may be needed close to the seating position for crutches, sticks or other walking aids to be 'parked' safely.

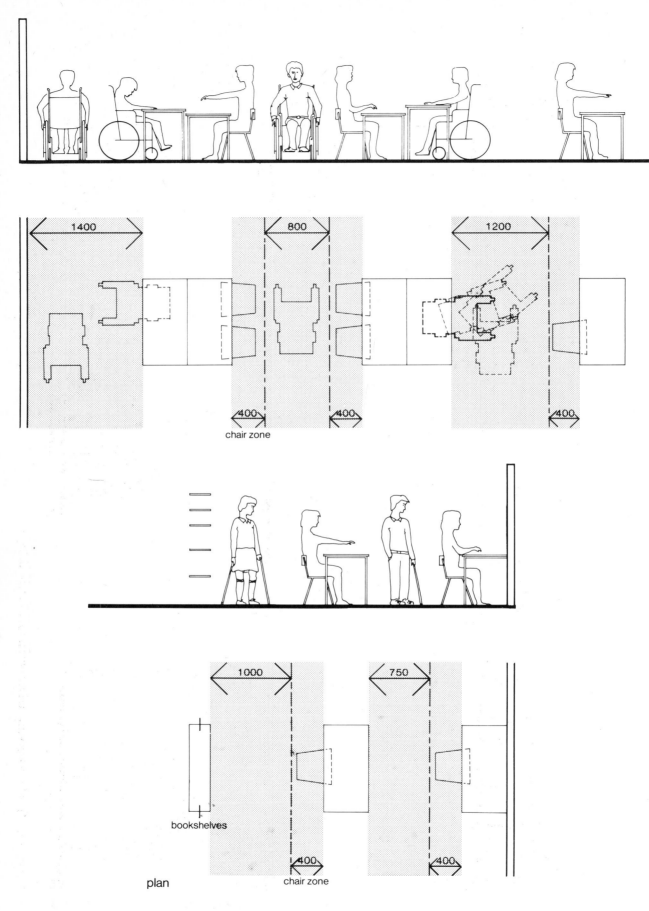

Figure A6. Guide to furniture spacings for disabled pupils

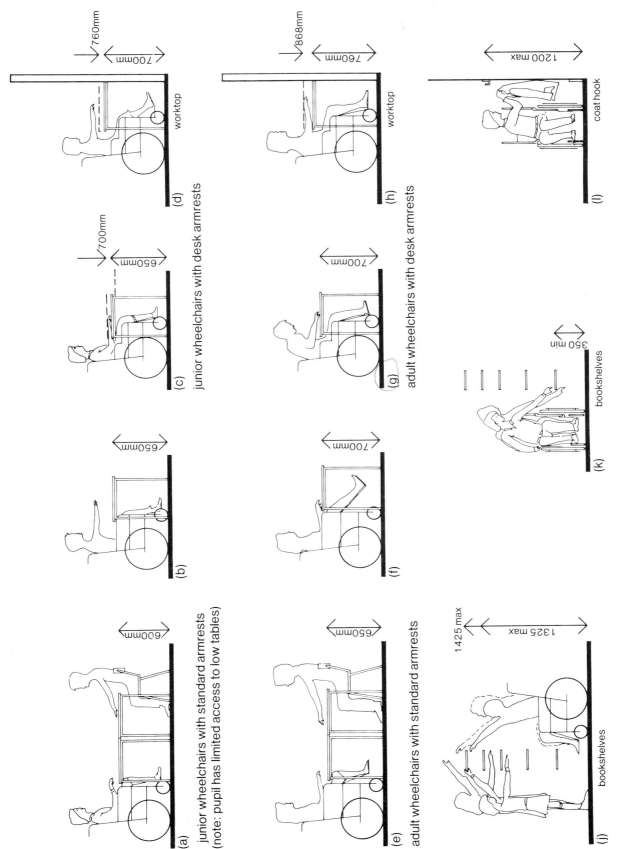

(a)

(b)

(c)

(d)

600mm

650mm

700mm

650mm

760mm

700mm

worktop

junior wheelchairs with standard armrests
(note: pupil has limited access to low tables)

junior wheelchairs with desk armrests

(e)

(f)

(g)

(h)

650mm

700mm

700mm

760mm

868mm

worktop

adult wheelchairs with standard armrests

adult wheelchairs with desk armrests

(j)

bookshelves

1425 max

1325 max

(k)

bookshelves

350 min

(l)

coat hook

1200 max

Figure A7.   Guide to working heights for pupils in wheelchairs

65

Workstations for typing/individual study

A.7   Figures A8 and A9 show two of the more common situations where appropriate space and furniture may be required for pupils with physical disabilities. In Figure A8, a writing surface approximately 700mm high is located to one side of a typing table (approximately 680mm high). The omission of a table leg as shown will benefit a pupil working from a wheelchair. Suitably positioned electric socket outlets are necessary for pupils using an electric typewriter or special equipment, and a larger work surface may be required where modified or remote controlled keyboards are used, for example with a microcomputer and visual display unit.

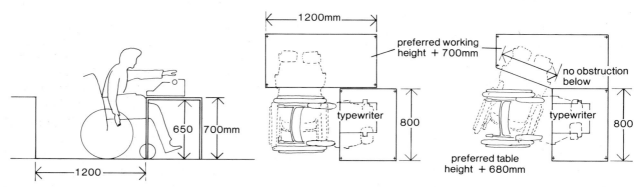

Figure A8.   Workspace for typing for pupils in a wheelchair (secondary school)

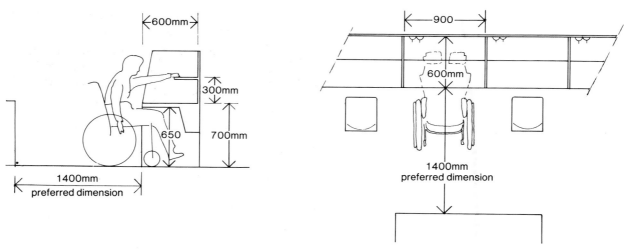

Figure A9.   Individual study carrel for pupils in a wheelchair (secondary school)

66

Bibliography

Architects and Building Group publications

Access for the Physically Disabled to Educational Buildings. Design Note 18, DES, 1979. (Revised edition in preparation.)

Acoustics in Educational Buildings. Building Bulletin 51, HMSO, 1975.

Building for Nursery Education. Design Note 1, DES, 1968.

ESN Schools: Designing for the Severely Handicapped. Design Note 10, DES, 1972.

Guidelines for Environmental Design and Fuel Conservation in Educational Buildings. Design Note 17 (revised edition), DES, 1981.

Lighting and Acoustic Criteria for the Visually Handicapped and Hearing Impaired in Schools. Design Note 25, DES, 1981.

Nursery Education in Converted Space. Building Bulletin 56, HMSO, 1978.

Nursery Education: Low Cost Adaptation of Spare Space in Primary Schools. Broadsheet 1, DES, 1980.

Other publications

Assessments and Statements of Special Educational Needs. Circular 1/83 (DES), HC (83)3/LAC(83)2 (DHSS).

Design of Educational Facilities for Deaf Children. *British Journal of Audiology,* Supplement No 3, February 1980. Royal National Institute for the Deaf.

Education (School Premises) Regulations 1981. SI No 909, HMSO, 1981.

Gazely, D. J. and Stone, P. T. *Visual Capacity, Lighting and Task Requirements of Partially Sighted Schoolchildren.* Light and Low Vision Report No 3 (and other publications), Vision and Lighting Research Group, Department of Human Sciences, University of Technology, Loughborough, 1981.

Goldsmith, S. *Designing for the Disabled* (third edition). RIBA Publications, 1976.

Hegarty, S., Pocklington, K. and Lucas, D. *Educating Pupils with Special Needs in the Ordinary School.* NFER-Nelson, 1981.

Hegarty, S., Pocklington, K. and Lucas, D. *Integration in Action: Case Studies in the Integration of Pupils with Special Needs.* NFER-Nelson, 1982.

Light for Low Vision. Chartered Institute of Building Services/The Partially Sighted Society, 1980.

Special Educational Needs. Report of the Committee of Enquiry into the Education of Handicapped Children and Young People (Warnock Report). Cmnd 7212, HMSO, 1978.

Department of Education and Science

A full list of free and priced publications produced by the Architects and Building Group is available free of charge from:

Department of Education and Science
Architects and Building Group
Room 7/38
Elizabeth House
York Road
London SE1 7PH

Printed in the UK for HMSO
Dd 137425 C40 9/84